FIELD GUIDE

to Living a Life of

COMMITMENT, COURAGE, and HONOR

10 Principles to Ignite Your Inner Compass

TAMARA SOLT

GREY POINT
PUBLISHING

Greybeard LLC
DBA Grey Point Publishing
www.greypointpublishing.com

Printed in the United States of America

10 9 8 7 6 5 4 3 2 1

ISBN: 979-8-988-1375-0-4
Library of Congress Control Number: 2023907034
E-book ISBN: 979-8-988-1375-1-1

Editing by Susan Reynolds
Copyediting by Lois Greenlee Stück
Proofreading by D. Baldogo
Cover and Book Interior Design by Susan Malikowski

For my daughters Daralyn and Kaitlyn. Never doubt your abilities; the world is yours for the taking.

To my mom for being a survivor.
And to my husband, Greg, who has always been my biggest cheerleader.

To all the incredible single mothers, women navigating through an uncharted maze of feeling lost or experiencing the challenges of a new divorce, and courageous women veterans searching for their path in this world, I want you to know that I've walked in your shoes. I want you to know that you are not alone in the struggles you are facing. I understand the journey you're on, and I have full confidence that you have the strength and determination to uncover your true desires and the most effective strategy for achieving them.

Believe in yourself, enjoy the journey, and know that you already possess all the resources necessary to design the life of your dreams. As you persevere and move forward, doors of opportunity will open. Never give up.

Contents

What I Learned as a United States Marine

COMPASS

Description: A compass is a finely tuned instrument used for guidance about where you are and where you want to go. If you fine-tune and follow your inner compass, you'll always be on the right path.

Mantras:

> I'm proud of how far I've come.
>
> I'm enjoying the journey and excited about my future.
>
> My life is meaningful and fulfilling.
>
> I am living each day in alignment with my authentic self.

Inspirational Song: "Unwritten," by Natasha Bedingfield. Nothing in the future has been written. It's up to you to author the story you want to pass down for generations to come. It's up to you to create your own happy ending.

How I Found My Internal Compass

I joined the United States Marines the moment I turned eighteen in January of 1984, without telling my parents, to escape an especially chaotic situation (living with an abusive alcoholic father). I felt guilty about leaving my younger brother and mother, but I needed out of that situation. I had been accepted to Ohio State University but chose to join the service in hopes of seeing the world, which felt bold albeit safer than remaining in Ohio. Three weeks after graduation, I arrived in Paris Island, South Carolina, as a U.S. Marine recruit.

In the 1980s, female Marines received different training than their male counterparts. Women were forbidden from holding combat roles, thus boot camp focused on physical conditioning, close-order drill, first aid, Marine Corps history and traditions, military customs and courtesies, the Uniform Code of Military Justice, uniform regulations, and water safety survival training. Leadership instruction was also an integral part of our training.

We learned to respond to orders, instructions, and commands. Teamwork was drilled into our heads. While some young women struggled, I had unknowingly longed for structure. I pushed hard, studied hard, and surprised even myself with how well I performed. Strangely enough, for the first time in my life I felt free.

After boot camp, I trained as a motor vehicle operator at Camp Lejeune in Jacksonville, North Carolina, where I learned how to drive a stick shift. I drove everything from an old military jeep to five-ton trucks.

After completing motor transport school, I shipped off to Camp Pendleton, California, to work in a motor pool. In 1985, the first-year female Marines were required to qualify with the M16 rifle, I discovered something unique about myself. Surprising everyone, especially myself, I shot a 240 out of a maximum 250 score on my first rifle qualification attempt, landing me in the Expert category.

Luckily, the Marine Corps wanted a few female rifle range instructors and offered me the chance to become a Primary Marksmanship Instructor (PMI). The hours were zero dark thirty in the morning until just before noon, in California, so hello beach afternoons!

Not long after, I qualified with a handheld gun and began splitting my time between the rifle and pistol ranges, teaching Marine Corps officers and enlisted personnel how to score high marks with a .45 or 9mm pistol.

Toward the end of 1985, I was selected to join the elite Marine Corps rifle and pistol team and consistently placed in the top three during competitions. Despite being the only female, I ranked second in a national rifle match held in Nevada where I used an M14 rifle to compete.

In 1987 I transferred to Okinawa, where I continued driving trucks and serving as a Primary Marksmanship Instructor. In 1988 I reenlisted for three more years and landed the Marine Corps Air Station at Kaneohe Bay, Hawaii, where I again served as a pistol range instructor. I also married and gave birth to my first daughter.

I spent seven years in the USMC and am proud to have been able to serve my country. I am grateful to the Marines for helping me gain a solid foundation of core values—commitment, courage, and honor—that I still use as my guideposts. They've been so instrumental in guiding my life that they provided the motivation for writing this book.

How the Marine Corps Core Values Changed My Life

For twelve years, I managed to bring up two healthy, strong, and self-reliant daughters as a single working mom. I worked hard to build a successful career with the federal government while pursuing my undergraduate and graduate degrees part-time. But once my girls had become teenagers and no longer required carpooling or my attendance at all cross-country and softball practices, I realized that it was time to refocus. Instead of executing a smooth transition, I suddenly found myself struggling to identify my passions, or who I wanted to be in this new phase of my life.

And this is why I wrote this *Field Guide*—for everyone feeling lost and confused while transitioning into something new. I've gone through that same experience, and I want to show you how using the core values I learned in the Marines—commitment, courage, and honor—helped me and can help you find your true purpose, embark on a journey of self-discovery, and create the change you want.

I not only used these core values to complete my undergraduate education while a working single mother, but also to earn an MBA. I later employed them to create at least six successful side hustles that not only paid living expenses but also paid for luxuries, including a portion of my children's college expenses and weddings. My side hustles included:

- Selling children's clothing on eBay when my daughters were young.

- Selling team-colored camouflage via a website.

- Refinishing furniture and flipping it for a profit.

- Selling vintage items on Etsy.

- Renting space at an antique mall to sell items.

- Co-founding a craft beer and wine bar.

Nothing ever came easy, but each side hustle added to my skillset, pushed me outside my comfort zone, and provided opportunities I would not have otherwise experienced. Each success bolstered my confidence and led to further exploration.

Let's discuss the three principles being a Marine taught me.

COMMITMENT

Commitment is the spirit of determination, dedication, perseverance, and teamwork. When you have a commitment mindset, you adopt a "never give up mentality," which will propel you through anything required to succeed, even when you feel unsure of your direction. Discipline is your driving force.

COURAGE

Courage is the mental strength and confidence that carries us through challenges and aids us in overcoming fear. Courage provides the inner strength to do what's right and the focus to adhere to higher standards.

HONOR

Honor is respecting others (including yourself!), acting responsibly, fulfilling obligations, and holding ourselves accountable for our actions.

We'll discuss how you can use these same core values to ignite your inner compass throughout this book.

How to Use This Book

This book is structured as an easy-to-read *Field Guide*, making it easy to identify the life-changing tasks you can address right now to find your own inner compass and thereby create a happy and productive future. We will discuss multiple ways you can discover your talents and passions, identify the core values that will drive your success, breach your comfort zone, and create a specific plan for marching forward. My heartfelt wish is to offer you ways to access the commitment, courage, and honor needed to identify your dream and follow it to create the life you most deeply desire.

Each chapter begins with an avatar symbol. It's a visual reminder of the chapter's central theme. Next, there will be a short list of mantras. A mantra is a word, phrase, or sound that is repeated either silently or aloud as a form of meditation or spiritual practice. Mantras are often recited repeatedly to focus the mind, induce a state of concentration or relaxation, and promote spiritual growth. They can be used as a tool to calm the mind, cultivate positive vibes, or connect with a higher power or inner self. Lastly, I present you with an inspirational song that is meant to get your soul in a high-vibe state. Listen to it before diving into each chapter for the perfect mindset. Let the music set the tone for your transformative journey.

Are you ready? Let's get started.

Principle # 1: Find Your Passions

TURTLE

Description: Finding your passions requires courage and work. Instead of comparing yourself to how others are progressing, trust that you'll get to where you need to be on your own time. Slow and steady often wins the race.

Mantras:

> I'm on the right track, give it time.
>
> I will be patient and trust in the journey.
>
> I give myself permission to explore whatever is calling me.
>
> Finding my true passion is worth the time and effort.

Inspirational Song: "Brand New Eyes," by Bea Miller. Often our underlying passions are frequently visible yet unnoticed. Looking at your life with a "new set of eyes" may be required. If you still can't see options, a close friend or significant other often sees what you can't see in yourself.

Opening Notes

During an afternoon auction, something shook deep within my soul: the quintessential "aha moment" that so many people spend a lifetime trying to find. When I discovered that I loved finding vintage items, it felt magical.

I want to show you how you can discover your own magical moments, but first let's discuss the difference between passion and purpose.

The Difference between Passion and Purpose

Merriam-Webster describes passion as "a strong liking or desire for, or devotion to some activity, object, or concept."

Simply put, passion is something you find for yourself, and purpose is something you give to the world. Passion is something you love (brings excitement), and purpose is a contribution that has meaning and impact. Those who are lucky can align their passions with their purpose.

When my husband and I owned Hop Yard 62, our craft beer and wine bar, one of the local musicians became a favorite act at our establishment. Jack (not his real name) also played at several venues around town, performing five or six nights a week, which limited his time with family. Over time, his passion for music began to wane. Some venues didn't want to pay him as much as he was worth, COVID hit, gas prices started to rise, and some establishments closed shop completely. Jack wondered if he should return to his old job managing a local restaurant.

Instead, Jack thought long and hard about what he wanted his music career to look like. Soon thereafter, he put a plan into action: He eliminated smaller establishments, while adding larger and more desirable venues that also paid more. He began playing at corporate events, which could be done during the day (benefitting his family life). He increased his fees so he could limit gigs to four nights per week. For the first time in his career, Jack made his own rules, reignited his passion, and felt he'd hit a grand slam. Instead of just going through the motions, he performed with more purpose, further fueling his passion. He was so much happier, and it showed.

One afternoon at a corporate performance, someone asked if he provided piano or guitar lessons. He'd never done so but decided to try. Six months later, Jack discovered that he loved working with young students. Jack not only discovered a completely new passion, he also found another income stream. Setting his parameters and performing his music with purpose ignited a new passion.

> *"The two most important days*
> *in your life are the day you are born and*
> *the day you find out why."*
>
> —**Mark Twain, author**

Discover Your Passion

Honestly, following your passions is easy; it's finding them that requires time and effort. Finding your passions can be a deeply personal and sometimes challenging process. When you see someone lucky enough to have found their passion, particularly when they've also been able to channel that passion into a dream career or side hustle, please remember this: that person likely embarked on his or her arduous journey feeling uncertain, insecure, and fearful—just as you'll likely feel along the way. Remember, passion-seeking journeys require the core values of courage, commitment, and honor.

To find your passion, you have to be a doer, an active participant in life, someone willing to try new things. Status quo won't get you there. You have to experiment as it's rarely a one-and-done experience. Sometimes you'll hate the new activity, and sometimes you'll see it as a joyful but unfulfilling experience you want to do only occasionally. Finding what really ignites your inner compass and gets your juices flowing will feel magical, make your inner compass's needle quiver toward the direction you now want to pursue further. The trick is hanging in there until you discover what makes your needle quiver.

Don't be discouraged if you haven't figured out what you're enthusiastic about yet. Many people have felt this way but then have found their passion—it just takes time. Curiosity is a great starting point.

> *"Passion for your work is a little bit of discovery, followed by a lot of development, and then a lifetime of deepening."*[1]
> —**Angela Duckworth, *Grit***

Take a Hard Look at Your Life

There are no real shortcuts to discovering your passion, but you can speed up the process by asking yourself tough questions that require self-reflection. If you don't already have one, buy yourself a journal, large enough for extended contemplation. Once you have your journal, find a quiet place that will encourage focused thinking and writing. If there are people at home, or other distractions, perhaps go to the library where it's quiet. Then, work your way through these exercises:

1. Ask yourself what kinds of thoughts fill your mind. Without judgment, write down everything that comes to mind, preferably in rapid succession. Set a timer and do this for three full minutes. When you are done, review your list to identify any patterns or themes. Circle anything that stands out.

2. Either go to or picture the books on your bookshelf. What types of books do you read or listen to most often? Which books do you love? What type of books constantly attract you in bookstores? Again, write it all down, and then review, looking for patterns.

3. Pull out your credit card and bank statements. What do you spend the most money on? Write down the types of things you obviously favor. For instance, do you spend the most money on travel or on donating to your favorite charity? When you review this list, do you see any obsessions? What we spend money on has a lot to do with what we value, which we'll discuss more later in the book.

4. Now write down the places you most often go. When out for the day, do you often stop at your favorite local flower shop? Is it because you just light up when you walk in? Do your senses delight when you smell the fresh aroma of the bou-

quet nearest the window? All these things are clues, and it's your job to start noticing. Imagine yourself as a detective. Instead of solving a crime, your job is to solve the mystery of your as-yet-unknown calling.

5. When you're at a party or gathering, which topics of conversation make you light up? When someone at a BBQ mentioned that she had a vintage clothing business on eBay, I lit up so much she showed me her collection, explained how she shopped Goodwill bins, and asked if I'd like to go with her sometime. We had an instant connection. Have you had something like this happen to you recently? It might indicate a hidden passion.

6. What do you get completely lost in? Is there an activity you do that becomes so pleasurable or engrossing that you lose track of time? Is there something you do that comes easily to you? Is there something you do so well that people often ask, "How'd you learn to do that?"

7. What activities bring you the most joy? Make a list of things you love to do. Don't leave anything out, no matter how trivial it may seem. If you really enjoy visiting the art museum on Sunday afternoons, write it down. If being near the ocean makes you feel amazing, write that down too. Love

working out? Write it down. The more you write down, the more themes will appear.

8. In our hyper-connected world, is there an activity you do that creates such a fervent desire to not be interrupted that you turn off your phone? Maybe when you are cooking a meal or baking a dessert, you put your phone on "do not disturb" because you don't want to be bombarded with constant text messages. Make a mental note of these moments.

9. Now think about your cultural values: What do you care about? What causes or issues are important to you? Passion often comes from a sense of purpose or a desire to make a difference in the world, so identifying your values can help you find what you're passionate about. What impact do you want to make in your small community or in the world at large?

And here's the biggest question of all: If money were no object, what would you spend your time doing? This is the biggest question because it's often the hardest to answer. We all create lives designed to support a lifestyle, our families, and our goals, but if you had enough money for all of those needs, what would you choose to do or become? Keep in mind that this is not a fantasy-fulfillment question, but a sincere question based on all the answers you provided in the nine questions above. Based on your core values and who you most want to be in this lifetime, what would you do with your precious time?

> **TIP**: Table any timelines you have in your head. Finding your passion takes time, and trying too hard may impede the process. Do all the journaling legwork, then let all those ideas percolate in your subconscious.

The Twelve Discovery Drive Journey

During my period of searching for a new life purpose, I created an idea I call my "Twelve Discovery Drive Journey." I decided to try one new activity each month (discovery) in the hope that trying something completely new—and out of my comfort zone (drive)—would help me discover the "aha moment" that sparked passion. Spoiler alert: it worked!

Because I had no idea what I was truly passionate about, I started at ground zero, which meant trying anything and everything, as long as it was new to me.

Metalsmithing

First, I tried metalsmithing. After researching online, I found affordable, weekly classes available at the Columbus Cultural Arts Center. I selected a jewelry-making class where I learned enough basic metalsmithing techniques to make a linked bracelet. The class description mentioned annealing, pickling, stamping, drilling, sawing/piercing, filing/sanding, plier usage, and patina—all of which were mostly foreign to me. Luckily, I had vowed not to allow fear to stop me, so I committed to simply listen, watch, and learn a new skill.

After a few weeks of instruction, we each received a two-by-four-inch piece of metal to work with. I decided on a bird/chick design I found online. When it came to cutting the birds out of the solid metal piece, we were given tiny saw blades. Being the novice, it took me more than three hours to saw and sand. I broke five blades in twenty minutes and went home with sore hands.

I thought about quitting but persisted (courage, commitment, and honor got me through). Today, when I wear that bracelet, I appreciate how hard I worked to make it. Ultimately, I decided that metalsmithing was not my thing, and that's okay because I learned the following:

- I enjoyed the creative process.

- I didn't enjoy working with small pieces and parts; the work felt tedious.

- Finishing a project felt satisfying and gave me a sense of accomplishment.

- I had the mental and emotional fortitude to give something I didn't like a genuine effort.

Screen Printing

Next I tried screen-printing, passing ink through a screen onto a physical object, such as a T-shirt, paper, or other surface. It involved transferring an image onto a stretched screen, enabling the artist to print multiple, identical copies of the image. I learned how to choose an image, prepare it, burn it onto a screen, and set it up for printing—a messier but far less tedious effort than metalsmithing jewelry. I liked it so much that I launched a mini line of screen-printed iPad and Messenger bags, which I sold on Etsy. I also learned the following about myself:

- Again, I enjoyed the creative process of screen printing.
- I loved it when someone liked my design so much that they purchased the item.
- It was fun and rewarding, but not my "aha moment."

Traveling Abroad

For my third new adventure of the year, I traveled to Rome, Italy. My husband won a prestigious award called the President's Club Award, which provided an all-expenses-paid trip to an upscale destination. Great minds think alike—and what perfect timing for my Twelve Discovery Drive quest.

I now had the opportunity to accompany my husband to one of the most beautiful and iconic countries on earth. I felt beyond ecstatic but nervous at the same time. I had questions and concerns:

- Can I get a passport in time?

- Is it safe?

- Do enough people in Italy speak English for me to feel at ease?

This adventure required courage, and I mustered it in time to visit so many places that made my soul happy. We crossed experiences off our bucket lists, such as visiting the Colosseum and the Vatican. We ate lots of gelato and pizza. After spending four days in Rome, we stopped in London for an additional three days before heading back home. My mindset shifted as a result of venturing so far outside of my normal routine and allowing myself to take in the sense of awe that was triggered by visiting all of these new places. My conclusions:

- From deep within my soul, I loved every second of flying across the ocean, visiting historic, cultural, and spiritual sites, trying exotic foods in charming restaurants, and meeting people different from me.

- This trip sparked my love of adventure.

- Experiences over things? *Hell yes.*
- I could overcome the fear of traveling far outside my comfort zone.
- Experiencing unfamiliar cultures felt expansive and rewarding.

In other words, I loved it. Travel as often as you can. Travel awakens your senses and opens your eyes to new opportunities, cultures, modes of transportation, food experiences, and history. Travel exercises your courage muscle by taking you outside of your comfort zone.

Need more convincing?

After tasting a new kind of creamy, full-fat yogurt while visiting her mother in Australia, Koel Thomae fell so deeply in love with it, she decided to bring that recipe to the U.S. Thirteen years later, Noosa Yoghurt landed on supermarket shelves. "You get into ruts. Travel automatically pushed me out of that rut," Thomae revealed.[2]

A trip to Haiti inspired Paul English to make enough money so he could meaningfully help the island's citizens. As a result of his passion for travel, he created the online travel search engine Kayak. "You're more alert when you travel," said English.[3]

My "Aha Moment" Finally Came

One day I suddenly wanted to attend a live auction. After searching the internet, I found an auction that sounded interesting only forty minutes away. Once there, I discovered two outdoor auctions occurring simultaneously. Household items were being auctioned off in the front; tools and furniture in the back. After obtaining my bidder number, I quickly saw a vintage Smith Corona typewriter I wanted, so I raised my hand for my first-ever auction bid. I wasn't going to stop until I won that great little piece of history. And then I heard those magic little words: "**SOLD** for $12.50 to the lady in the long black dress." I had won.

I won three more lots/items before I headed home, but it was that first win that created my "aha moment." I literally felt excitement, joy, and wonder coursing through my body. This, I realized, was the passion I had been chasing for so long.

"*Passion is energy. Feel the power that comes from focusing on what excites you.*"

—Oprah, media mogul

I immediately acted on my passion and attended auctions weekly for a year. I opened an Etsy shop and a small vendor booth at a local antique mall to sell the treasures I found. Both generated extra work, but my passion for discovering and sharing vintage items made it so much fun I never felt tired. Although my husband had pointed out long before that I loved finding little treasures at the thrift stores, I had ignored any thoughts about doing something with that passion until that "aha moment" at the auction. I learned not to ignore what I like to do, as well as the following:

- An "aha moment" evokes strong feelings of excitement and joy. You'll know it when you feel it.

- A passion for vintage had been part of my thrifting instincts, but I'd missed it.

- Someone close to me saw something valuable that I far-too-easily dismissed.

- Trying something new often yields unexpected results.

How did I really find my passion? I lived life. I didn't stay home and watch television or waste hours on social media. I left my house and chose a series of small, explorative adventures. I had no expectations beyond adventure. I simply focused on paying attention as I lived in the moment—and it paid off.

Watch for Signs You're on the Right Path

Besides venturing into the larger world and exploring activities, you can dig deep and become more self-aware of the skills you currently possess. Often these skills are evident in your day-to-day interactions, but you've grown so used to doing them you don't see them as passions. Ask your husband, boyfriend, girlfriend, wife, or close friend because they probably see where you excel long before you do.

When you are traveling in the right direction, serendipitous occurrences will awaken something that had been sleeping in some dark corner of your psyche. They may feel like mere coincidence yet actually be a sign that you are going down the right path. New opportunities will present themselves and new people will randomly appear in your life. Stay open, remain alert, and be ready to receive. Commit yourself to the task of taking risks to discover your true passions. After all, the greatest way to honor yourself is to know yourself.

Remember that finding your passions is a journey, not a destination. It will likely require time and effort, but the process of exploring and discovering what brings you joy and fulfillment can be a deeply rewarding experience.

Closing Notes

Try new things monthly. Invest in new skills and knowledge by taking classes or trying new activities. Find a new hobby. Pay attention to the thoughts that occupy your mind, where you spend money, what you get completely lost in. What do you love to do? What are you good at? Dig deep and focus on what excites you. Get off the couch. Live life. Journal.

Find Your Passions Exercises

Now it's time for you to create your own Twelve Discovery Drive roadmap. Start with any month you like,
then write down something new to do. Examples might
include take a class, attend a musical, run a 5k race, or
anything you might like to try. With each new event,
you will discover more about what makes you tick.
You'll love some events and dislike others, but that's the
point. Each step brings you closer to finding your "aha
moment."

Grab your journal, or use the space below, to jot down
ideas for what you'll try each month.

January _____

February _____

March _____

April _____

May _____

June _____

July _____

August _____

September _____

October _____

November _____

December _____

Once you find a couple of events or classes to attend, *commit* to going. No excuses. If you're hesitant to go solo, invite a friend along. Feel good about being courageous enough to explore territory that breeches your comfort zone. Honor your journey by tackling each new adventure with gusto. Enjoy and look forward to the changes and opportunities that are sure to come your way.

Lastly, I'd like you to be a little creative in the remaining space below (or in your journal). It's time to get a little silly and do something you may already do when you are bored. I want you to doodle. Doodling is the act of making random, incoherent marks for no particular reason other than that it makes you feel like a kid again. Patterns, themes, and recurring symbols are common occurrences in doodling. So grab a pen or pencil and start doodling away. Look for any themes that might stand out.

Principle #2: Discover Your Strengths and Talents

HUMMINGBIRD

Description: A hummingbird has an inner superpower that allows him to hover until food is secured. Begin by finding *your* inner superpowers. Once you know what your strengths and talents are, you can focus on the right kind of jobs and opportunities.

Mantras:

I am discovering my inner superpowers.

I have many talents and gifts to offer the world.

Once I embrace my strengths and talents, I will soar.

Every day is a new opportunity to discover what makes me special.

Inspirational Song: "Hero," by Mariah Carey. Focus on being your own hero. Work hard and persevere in your quest to find out who you really are, which fine-tunes your internal compass.

Opening Notes

It took me a long time to realize that my strength wasn't in shooting a rifle and becoming an expert marksman. My ability to focus was my strength, which I have been able to use my entire life. After all, talent can only take you so far.

We are all blessed with unique talents and abilities. When you discover and use those strengths, you become your most effective and most fulfilled self, which is the ideal way to honor yourself and others. But identifying your strengths and talents isn't always easy.

The Difference between Strengths and Talent

First, we need to differentiate strengths from talent. You may have a natural talent for shooting a rifle and hitting the bullseye, but it's your focus that enables you to calm your breathing and gently pull back on the trigger, confident the rifle will not accidentally fire and make a startling noise. Focus is your strength.

A strength is something you do well, no matter the task. You probably have an excellent track record with this strength, and others may recognize you for it. If the strength is being exercised, you feel as if you're "in the zone" or blissfully lost in whatever you are doing.

Let's continue with the focus example. I discovered I was fiercely accurate at shooting a rifle and a pistol in my early twenties as a U.S. Marine. As you read at the beginning of the book, superiors selected me to shoot on the Marine Corps' rifle and pistol team. I didn't know I had exceptional focus, but once I linked my ability to that strength, I used it repeatedly during major life events. I used it to earn a degree while a working, single parent. I used it again in my forties to start a company with my husband. We opened a craft beer and wine bar in our town with zero experience and successfully ran that business for almost six years, while also working full-time jobs. We committed to the journey, courageously faced our fears, focused on what needed to be done, and worked hard to honor our commitment to ourselves and those who believed in us. Looking back on my life, I can see many more examples. When you pinpoint your strengths, your confidence grows, and the possibilities are endless.

Discover Your Strengths and Talents

To identify your unique strengths and talents, it's often helpful to look backwards. Here are three techniques to help identify yours:

1. Review your current resume. Circle (or list) all strengths you gained in current and past jobs. Look for special projects you've worked on or moments in your career when you felt most proud of your work. What you've accomplished is a roadmap of strengths and an indicator of how much you've grown.

2. Consider your favorite activities as a child or teen.

Maybe you loved drawing or music (which reflects creativity). Maybe you stood up for a friend who was being teased (which reflects bravery). Or maybe you always enjoyed planning family events (which reflects planning and organizational strength).

3. List the types of challenges that consistently attract you. Do you want to organize your friend's closet every time you go to her house? Your strength may be organization. Are you the type who never gives up no matter what? Your strength might be determination and perseverance.

Consider Your Past Commitments

It also helps to revisit past commitments and what they may have taught us. For example, I chose to become a U.S. Marine. The military provided me with a solid foundation and revealed (or developed) a lengthy list of strengths, including:

- Entrepreneurial spirit. I had to learn how to get things done, often with insufficient guidance or little supervision.

- Lifelong learner. I had to learn and learn fast—to the point that I grew to love learning and gained a lot of confidence from it.

- Loyalty. I took an oath and stood by it. It's a helpful strength in life.

- Integrity. If I didn't have it going in, I owned it going out. I used it to honor my own life and fulfill all required duties.

- Strong work ethic. I learned how to focus and work efficiently. This serves me well in everything I take on.

- Initiative. I learned how to think for myself and take action when required.

- Discipline. That military discipline becomes pure gold in everyday life.

- Responsibility. I honor myself and others in everything I attempt.

What past commitments have you been involved in? What strengths did you develop as a result? For instance, maybe you coached your son or daughter's little league team. Think about the strengths you had to either possess or develop to take on such a task. Coaches embody such strengths as being positive, supportive, observant, patient, respectful, and committed.

Find Your Reflected Best Self

In an article titled "How to Play to Your Strengths," authors Laura Morgan Roberts, Gretchen Spreitzer, Jane Dutton, Robert E. Quinn, Emily D. Heaphy, and Brianna Barker created an exercise to help participants tap into their hidden talents as a way to increase career potential.

They call this finding your "Reflected Best Self (RBS)."[4] Here's the basic concept:

a. To begin, gather input from family, friends, colleagues, or teachers by asking them what they see as your key strengths. Ask for specific examples. Tell them that you're not fishing for compliments but truly want objective opinions on what they see as your most potent abilities. In this step, send an email or letter so the person has time to think before they respond.

b. Search for common themes in the feedback. In this step, it might be best to copy the information into a table or spreadsheet. Look for consistency or contradictions. Note anything surprising.

c. Use the summarized information and what you know about your own strengths to write a description of yourself. Start the description with: "When I am at my best, I . . . " Instead of bullet points, write two to four paragraphs that describe your best self.

d. In light of the information you've gathered and summarized, you should now reconsider the ideal job description you'd like to have or the long-term objectives you want to achieve. Last but not least, you should ask yourself, "What positives can I take away from this new information?"

Discovering and tapping into your hidden talents is an empowering journey of self-discovery and personal growth. By embracing curiosity, experimenting with different activities, seeking feedback, and maintaining a growth mindset, you can unleash your full potential. Embrace the adventure of self-discovery, and you will uncover an extraordinary world of hidden talents within yourself. This discovery is just the start, applying your strengths is the real game changer.

Try an Online Assessment

If you still need help coming up with a list of strengths, you can find online assessments that may help. My favorite is *Clifton Strengths Finder 2.0*. This popular tool can be taken online for less than $50. Their tool delineates thirty-four strengths, which they measure based on how you think, feel, and behave. The results report gives you insights into your most powerful themes. Your top five are your most powerful natural talents, your inner superpowers. To take this test, go to https://www.gallup.com/cliftonstrengths.

When I took this assessment, my top five strengths were Focus, Learner, Responsibility, Discipline, and Maximizer. While the first four are, for the most part, self-explanatory, Maximizer is defined by several qualities. This stood out for me: "By nature, you forge ahead to build the life you envision. You reach your goals by finding as many opportunities as possible to use your unique abilities and natural gifts." This statement proved so powerful I now use it as my personal goal mantra.

The assessment also provides actions you can take to maximize your potential and explains how to identify blind spots. Once you know your strengths, you can use this knowledge to focus on finding work or projects that allow your strengths to shine.

Consider Your Younger, Wiser Self

Some of the strengths and skills that we possess as adults are the consequence of efforts we began as adolescents. During most of my childhood, I practically lived at the West Side Boys and Girls Clubs of Columbus where I learned how to play sports, shoot billiards, play foosball and air hockey, cheerlead, swim, create ceramic pieces, as well as to value sportsmanship, responsibility, and competition. I even got my first real job there, checking kids in at the front desk. During that time, I received two citations, both of which recognized the qualities I was busy developing and both of which significantly elevated my sense of accomplishment and self-esteem.

Now it's your turn. Find a quiet place in your house and take the next twenty minutes to reflect back on your childhood. No matter what type of environment you grew up in, there will be moments of strength and courage that stand out. What were some of your talents as a child? Where did you excel? If you can't remember, ask a parent or close relative who knew you well. Don't leave your quiet space until you've come up with a few ideas. You can expand on this idea in the exercise at the end of the chapter.

Discovering your strengths and talents is a transformative journey that can unlock your true potential and reshape your life. The power of self-awareness and understanding your unique abilities cannot be underestimated. By recognizing and embracing your strengths and talents, you cultivate confidence, engagement, and a deep sense of purpose. As you align your life with your natural talents, you not only experience personal fulfillment but also make significant strides towards achieving your goals, honoring yourself, and making a positive impact on the world around you. So, take the time to explore your strengths, embrace your uniqueness, and unlock the incredible potential within you.

Closing Notes

Find your inner superpowers. Talents are natural. Strengths are what you develop and maximize. Stay focused and committed. What kind of challenges are you attracted to? What are you good at doing? Ask friends or colleagues for feedback. Take an online assessment. Look back through your childhood.

Discover Your Strengths and Talents Exercises

Begin by reviewing your resume to pinpoint strengths you've developed at work. Circle trends and look for clues for hidden strengths.

Use your journal to answer the following questions:

- Think back on your childhood and early adolescence. What did you excel at doing? What did you love to do? What won you accolades?

- Ask three or more trusted friends and/or your spouse what specific strengths they think you possess.

- What type of challenges are you attracted to and why?

- What are your hobbies?

- What do you do better than others?

Principle # 3: Determine Your Personal Values

DOG

Description: Dogs epitomize loyalty, patience, love, protection, fidelity, and faith. These qualities are a dog's inner compass. Once you know your personal values well enough to fine-tune your inner compass, making important and tough decisions will become much easier.

Mantras:

I will show kindness to a stranger today.

A positive transformation is happening within me.

I love the person I am becoming.

My intuition is strong. When I have an instinct about something, I listen to it.

Inspirational Song: "Born This Way," by Lady Gaga. Follow her lead in being and becoming your authentic self, being the bold and brave person who honors her values.

Opening Notes

In the simplest form, values are guideposts for your actions and decisions. Values are individual beliefs that guide you at every turn, like a compass. They are the unwritten rules that set standards of behavior in our everyday life.

Understanding and embracing our personal beliefs is critical in the pursuit of a meaningful and successful life. Personal values act as a compass, guiding our decisions, defining our priorities, and influencing our behavior. By diving into and discovering our own set of beliefs and values, we unleash a powerful tool that allows us to live an authentic and purpose driven life.

Beliefs are what we generally hold to be true, without proof or evidence. For instance, you may believe stealing or cheating on your spouse is wrong, regardless of the circumstances. Our beliefs grow from what we see, hear, read, experience, and think about. We can believe something but not act on it. However, we derive our more deeply ingrained values from our beliefs.

Our values translate into attitudes and behaviors, how we treat others and approach situations. We learn our values through a combination of instruments, including how we grew up, family traditions, experiences, education systems, and our environment.

Even if you've never identified or written down what you believe your values to be, we all have a set of values we live by. It's your everyday actions and how you respond to events in life that will reveal your true core values.

Let's say you're on the elevator and you see an individual rushing toward the elevator door just as it is beginning to close. Would you choose to hold the door open for them? Or, if you're running late, would you let the door close? If you held the door open, whether you were in a hurry or not, one of your values might be kindness. Because your internal compass points to kindness, you would almost always hold the door open.

If you value helping others, you might always be that person who volunteers to coach your child's soccer team or are only interested in working for a company that has a positive impact on people in the local community.

The scenarios above are reflections of your personal beliefs and values. Your core values are fundamental beliefs about your life that guide you in the day-to-day decision-making process. Because of these values, those decisions are usually made without hesitation. When you aren't sure what your values are, you become more reactive to daily challenges and choices and have a harder time making decisions.

Common Personal Values

Sometimes it helps to have a list to peruse. Below is a list of values. Circle the ones you recognize in yourself in black, then circle the ones you'd most like to develop in red. Give thought to how each of these values affect the decisions you make about your life. Pinpoint the values that you will commit to honoring, and write the list in your journal, along with your commitment to honor them.

Accountability	Exploration	Personal time
Achievement	Expressiveness	Physical challenge
Adventure	Fairness	Pleasure
Ambition	Faith	Positivity
Art	Family	Power
Assertiveness	Financial security	Practicality
Balance	Fitness	Preparedness
Beauty	Focus	Privacy
Belonging	Freedom	Problem solving
Boldness	Friendship	Professionalism
Calmness	Fun	Public service
Carefulness	Goodness	Quality
Challenge	Hard work	Recognition

Change	Health	Relationship
Cheerfulness	Helping others	Relaxation
Commitment	Honesty	Reliability
Community	Honor	Resourcefulness
Compassion	Humility	Respect
Competence	Improvement	Responsibility
Competitiveness	Independence	Results-oriented
Consistency	Influencing others	Risk-taking
Contentment	Ingenuity	Security
Contribution	Inquisitiveness	Serenity
Control	Insightfulness	Self-care
Cooperation	Integrity	Self-control
Correctness	Intelligence	Self-development
Courtesy	Intuition	Selflessness
Creativity	Joy	Service
Curiosity	Justice	Simplicity
Decisiveness	Knowledge	Spirituality

Democracy	Leadership	Spontaneity
Dependability	Legacy	Stability
Determination	Love	Strength
Diligence	Loyalty	Structure
Discipline	Making a difference	Success
Diversity	Mastery	Teamwork
Effectiveness	Meaningful work	Thoroughness
Efficiency	Minimalism	Thoughtfulness
Elegance	Money	Timeliness
Empathy	Nature	Tolerance
Enjoyment	Openness	Uniqueness
Equality	Order	Unity
Ethics	Originality	Usefulness
Excellence	Participation	Vitality
Excitement	Perfection	Wealth
Expertise	Personal growth	Wisdom

Eight Ways to Determine Your Personal Values

If you are unsure what you value most, find a pen and paper, or better yet, your journal, and work your way through the following prompts:

1. List specific people you most admire. List any role models. These could be famous people, your parents, people in your community, someone you've worked for in the past, or even characters from a book you love. What are the qualities you most admire about them? Make a list and then evaluate where you fall on possessing each admirable trait. What qualities do they possess, or what behaviors would you like to adopt as your own?

2. Recall a specific time during the last six months when something happened and you took a stand, or when something happened and failure to act bothered you to the core. What do these moments reveal about your core values? What do they reveal about how you are doing upholding your core values? You might find that whatever rubbed you the wrong way is in direct opposition to your values.

3. Now think again about the last six months. What did you spend the most time doing? Where did you spend the most money? If you spent a lot on

fitness attire and gym memberships, you value health and wellness. If you booked trips three or four times a year, you value adventure and having fun. You can extract a host of clues from looking at where you spend your hard-earned money.

4. Imagine that you have created a fictional world where absolutely everything, from the way in which its inhabitants relate to one another to the kinds of commodities and services that are accessible to them, is entirely at your disposal. What sorts of behaviors might you anticipate? What behavior would you reward? What actions would receive punishment? The more in-depth you think about this exercise, the more you will reveal your core values based on your ideal world.

5. When do you feel most like yourself during the day? Is it when you volunteer at the dog shelter? Is it when you're working out or gardening? Maybe it's when you're talking about human rights or childcare issues. Is there anything you get lost in or lose track of time while doing? When you're in situations that allow you to be your authentic self, that's a clue that you are in alignment with your core values. If it feels wrong, then it's probably a situation in opposition to your values. In situations where you feel like your true authentic

self, what's going on? Write down what activity is happening, your emotions, and who you're with.

6. Recall the most meaningful moments in your life and what made those moments special to you. It could be something you completed that made you feel extremely proud. List these moments, and themes will emerge.

7. What types of stories most inspire you? What types of stories resonate with you? These can be stories you read in a book, stories you see on the news, or even a story a friend told you. We're all drawn to certain types of stories. For instance, I love movies and stories based on true events, as the characters usually show resiliency or some risk-taking or self-awareness, which I value.

8. What compliment do you hear most often? Even if you tend to brush off compliments, they can be instructive. People value what they see as your most potent contributions.

Now that you've learned more about your personal values, let's dig a little deeper.

Extract Your Top Core or Personal Values

In Jenny Blake's book *Pivot*, she discusses value mining, then uses a mind-mapping exercise to extract her top values.[5] To do this, go through your responses to all eight questions above and circle any key words or phrases that jump out at you. Do you feel anything is missing? If so, write it down. For instance, if you believe you value creativity but that was not a word or phrase from any answer above, still write it down.

Write the word "values" in the center of a blank page. Now take each word or phrase that you extracted from the exercise above and space them evenly in a circular formation around the word "values." Next, draw lines from the word "values" to each of these phrases. It should look something like a spiderweb.

Now, from each of your phrases, jot down how they are showing up in your life today or why it's important to you. For instance, when I did this exercise with Health/Wellness as a value, this was how I decided to manifest this value in my life:

- I choose to walk two miles a day.
- I go hiking or biking.
- I take yoga classes.
- I play pickleball.

I could go on and on with this one because I value health. Following is an illustration of a *mind map* (we'll discuss other ways to use them in Principle #6 on goal setting).

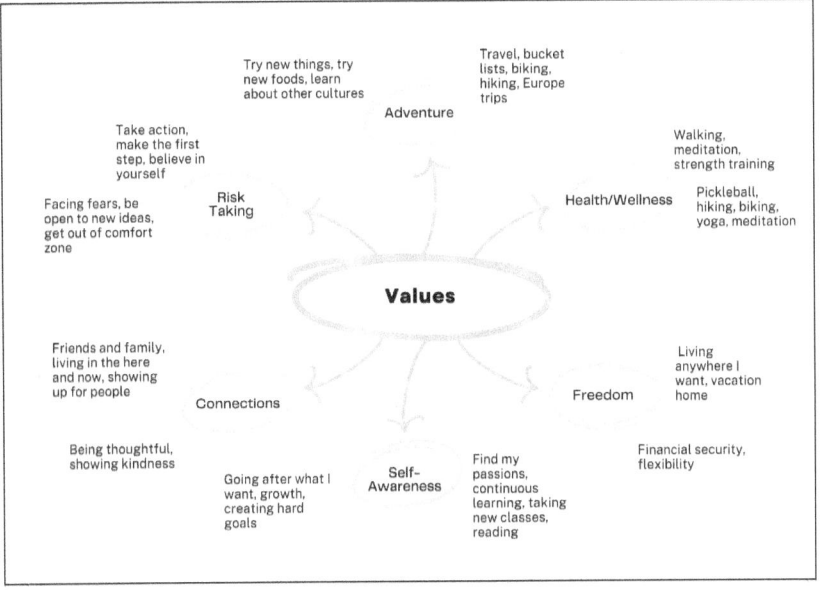

Try new things, try new foods, learn about other cultures

Travel, bucket lists, biking, hiking, Europe trips

Adventure

Take action, make the first step, believe in yourself

Walking, meditation, strength training

Facing fears, be open to new ideas, get out of comfort zone

Risk Taking

Health/Wellness

Pickleball, hiking, biking, yoga, meditation

Values

Friends and family, living in the here and now, showing up for people

Living anywhere I want, vacation home

Connections

Freedom

Being thoughtful, showing kindness

Financial security, flexibility

Going after what I want, growth, creating hard goals

Self-Awareness

Find my passions, continuous learning, taking new classes, reading

Mind Map Diagram

Map out your values and then use a distinct color pen or a highlighter to highlight the values most important to you. A straightforward way to help you narrow this list is to ask yourself: If I had to make a decision today, which value would I base that decision on? For example, if a friend asks whether I'd like to go out for a drink with her and a few friends after work today at 4 p.m., I might ask myself, "Have I worked out yet?" (I value health and wellness). If the response is no, I may respond to my friend and inform her that I can meet them at 5 p.m. so that I can get a forty-minute walk in first. One of my core values guided my decision.

Now that you have mapped out some of your values, pick your top three to five values.

> **TIP**: If you need help with a list of values, use the list at the beginning of the chapter or Google "core values."

Make Your Values Uniquely Yours

Now here's the fun part. Take those top three to five values and change them into something fun and easy to remember.[6] Doing this makes them uniquely yours. For instance, when I did this exercise, my top five values were health, adventure, self-awareness/learning, relationships, and risk-taking. Here's how I made them uniquely mine.

- For Health, I changed it to **Stay Solt Strong** (Solt is my last name). How it manifests: Do something daily to keep my body and mind strong. Play pickleball, walk, bike, strength train, stretch, do yoga, meditate, and remain active. I will honor myself, my body, and my mind.

- For Adventure, I changed it to **Be a Bucket List Buster**. How it manifests: Live adventurously, try new things, see novel places, ride my bike, hike, go on cruises, and travel the world. I will have the courage to try new things.

- For Relationships, I changed it to **Be a Good Human**. How it manifests: Connections are everything. Be a friend to keep a friend. Let go of people who bring me down. Strive to be a devoted friend, mom, wife, daughter, and grandma. Always be thoughtful and kind. I will show commitment to others.

- For Self-Awareness and Learning, I changed it to **Know Thyself**. How it manifests: I will continue to get to know myself. Never stop learning, read daily, take new and interesting classes, and be creative. I will commit to keeping my mind sharp.

- And lastly, for Risk Taker, I changed it to **YOLO** (an acronym for *you only live once*). How it manifests: Live big and take risks. Face fears and get out of my comfort zone often. I will strive to always show commitment, courage, and honor in all that I do.

I suggest writing your inspirational phrases and commitments down or typing them into your computer, but most importantly, make sure you review them often. These are your guiding values, the pinpoints on your personal compass that make decision-making easier.

If you genuinely want to live a life of commitment, courage, and honor, focus on living every day according to your values. When you are aware of your values, and your actions and behaviors are in harmony with them, you can live each day as your most authentic self.

Decisions will come more easily, and you will have a greater sense of peace.

Closing Notes

Our values are our attitudes, behaviors, and how we treat others and approach situations. Strengthen your internal compass. Follow your true north. Seek out role models. Get to know your authentic self. What are some of your proudest or most meaningful moments? Create a mind map. Make your values uniquely yours.

Determine Your Personal Values Exercises

Review your answers to the eight questions from the section titled "Eight Ways to Determine Your Personal Values."

- What have you learned about your core values?

- Write down any core values you want to develop.

- Write a commitment statement to develop those core values.

- List ways to manifest the desired values in your everyday life.

- In the space below or in your journal, take your top values and make them uniquely yours.

Principle #4: Face Your Fears

KOI FISH

Description: In Japan, koi fish represent strength and perseverance. At some point in our lives, we all have to show determination, strength, perseverance, tenacity, and courage. Your time is now.

Mantras:

I will endure any discomfort, knowing it won't last long.

I am moving past fear in order to grow.

I am feeling the fear and doing it anyway.

I have all the courage I need.

Inspirational Song: "Brave," by Sara Bareilles. It's your time to shine and be the brave person I know you can be.

Opening Notes

We all get comfortable with our routines and habits. The only way you can experience true magic is to try something outside those routines and habits. There will be risk. There will be fear and anxiety. Most importantly, there will be growth. It's time to get a little uncomfortable and punch fear in the face.

Everyone has his or her own version of a comfort zone where they feel most at home. It's a safe environment where we can anticipate our reactions, behaviors, and emotions in response to any given activity, circumstance, person, or experience. Your comfort zone is not a physical location; rather, it is a mental state in which everything in your environment has its proper place and everything is going exactly to plan.

Whenever I entered the craft beer bar I owned with my husband, I went straight to the bar and sat down. My husband went to each table and engaged in conversation with customers. Some of those people he knew, and others he didn't know. Sitting at the bar was my comfort zone; interacting with customers was his comfort zone.

Does this describe you? You always order the same Starbucks coffee in the morning, adhere to the same routine at the gym, and take the same route home. You've been in the same profession for almost a decade, and the mere idea of doing something else keeps you awake at night. As you can see, our comfort zones can be quite restricting; therefore, occasionally stepping outside of it can be a productive method to promote personal and professional growth. Yes, it requires commitment, and courage, and honor.

The Comfort Zone

Management guru Judith Bardwick defined the phrase "comfort zone" in her 1991 work *Danger in the Comfort Zone* as "a behavioral state within which a person operates in an anxiety-neutral condition, using a limited set of behaviors to deliver a steady level of performance, usually without a sense of risk."[7]

Comfort zones have their purpose, but leaving one's comfort zone is what often leads to extraordinary discoveries. Leaving your comfort zone may be necessary for you to reach your full potential. If doing something new induces fear within you, that's okay. Fear can signal that you're about to learn something new. Facing down that fear is a courageous thing to do, and we all know by now that being courageous is primary to living your best life. Let's be courageous together!

The following graphic depicts the various comfort zone stages and what happens at each stage as you begin to step out of it.

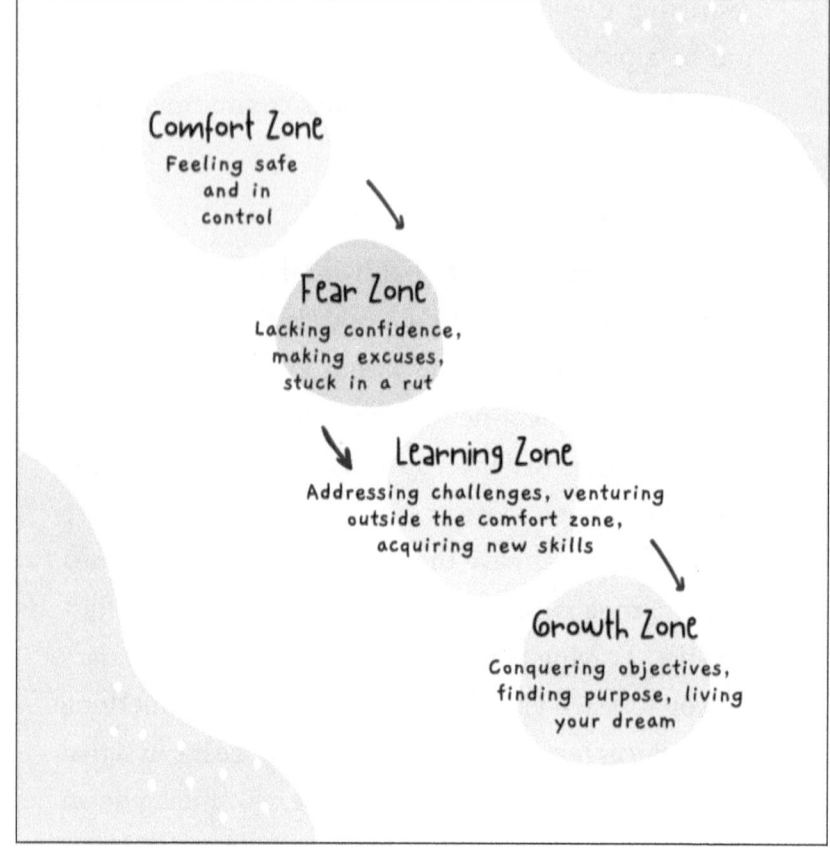

Comfort Zone Diagram

Stepping out of the comfort zone, you enter the dreaded fear zone. Besides fear, you will find reasons (excuses) as to why you should stay put. You may lack self-confidence to some degree, or you may be worried about what other people might think.

If you are courageous enough to take that first step out of the fear zone, you will enter the learning zone, where you begin learning new skills and facing new challenges, but you are willing to try them. Finally, you enter the growth zone, where the magic happens. Here, you begin to see a whole new side of yourself. This is where you start finding hidden talents and purpose and start setting goals.

Staying in your comfort zone for extended periods with the same morning ritual, eating the same peanut butter sandwich for lunch, and seeing the same people every day eventually leads to autopilot. It may feel exhilarating, and most of all, comfortable, but being caught in the same old routine is limiting. You risk getting stuck in a rut where life becomes boring and predictable, or you remain paralyzed by fear, which robs you of reaching your full potential.

Beware the Dreaded 'F Word'

Fear may be the worst "F word" in our vocabulary. Fear stops us in our tracks and holds us back. What level of fear are you experiencing? Are you too afraid to take those first steps? When I started writing this book, I didn't know where to start and feared I did not have the ability to complete it. To overcome the fear, I simply started writing. Though painful to do, writing felt better than doing nothing at all. While pounding out words, I developed faith the rest would come—if I could tamp down doubts and fears and trust the process and my inner compass. I also tamped down fear by asking myself: What's the best that could happen if I write this book? I could create a book that helps people live a life of commitment, courage, and honor, which would make me happy and help my readers. What's the worst that could happen if I do not write this book? I will regret that I never tried. Which would you choose?

You *Are* Smart Enough

Many individuals also fear inadequacy. I've uttered "I'm not smart enough" a thousand times throughout my lifetime. When I learned that you become what you constantly repeat in your thoughts, I committed to altering my internal and external narrative by writing and saying: "I am *more* than smart enough. I am creative, confident, and adept at problem-solving." This type of affirmation is a way to courageously honor yourself. Reinforcing it will help you overcome fear.

. . . .

Here's a little secret; Regardless of how others may present themselves on social media, nobody has it all figured out.

. . . .

If you're nervous about making mistakes or failing, that's normal. Making mistakes and failing is a necessary part of learning. The emotion of fear can motivate us to achieve our wildest dreams and hardest goals. Imagine a baby who has spent time crawling and is now trying to take their first steps. They get up, take one step, and fall, and they do this repeatedly until they succeed. The idea here is to reframe your efforts as tiny steps. If you fall, it's okay because you can trust that "walking" will come. Success is inevitable—if you keep trying. Stay committed and courageous and your life will start taking the shape you envision.

Listen to Yourself, Not Others

We all have an irrational fear of external judgment. What will my family think? What will my friends or co-workers think? Do you know what I say to that? Who cares. You do you, and I'll do me. Period, end of discussion. In *The Top Five Regrets of the Dying*, Bronnie Ware revealed the most common regret dying people expressed: "I wish I had had the courage to live a life true to myself, not the life others expected of me."[8]

> *"Fear is good. Like self-doubt, fear is an indicator. Fear tells us what we have to do.... The more scared we are of a work or calling, the surer we can be that we have to do it.... If it means nothing to us, there'd be no resistance."*
>
> **—Steven Pressfield, *The War of Art*[9]**

Let that sink in. Fear can have a positive effect. Fear can be your friend.

Leave Your Comfort Zone

There are many benefits to leaving your comfort zone, pushing past your fears, and taking small risks:

- It is the highest honor you can give yourself.

- It can give you a mental health boost because you are committing to something out of the ordinary.

- It supports personal growth by teaching you about your interests, passions, talents, strengths, and weaknesses.

- It allows you to see different perspectives.

- It makes you more creative by taking your mind off autopilot.

- It makes you more resilient and adaptable.

- It's the perfect boredom buster. When life becomes much more interesting and worth getting out of bed for, you will feel happier.

- It makes you more confident. Each time you accomplish something you didn't think you were capable of, you become more confident, knowledgeable, and skilled.

- It naturally makes you courageous. Tackling the

unknown and proving to yourself you can push past your boundaries and limiting self-beliefs reinforces confidence and self-esteem.

- It widens your social circle. Stepping out of your comfort zone, discovering who you are, and overcoming your fears will ultimately result in new and better relationships.

Getting out of your comfort zone and taking even small risks helps you see yourself in a more positive and proactive light. Surviving a calculated risk bolsters self-confidence and reinforces a belief that you can handle whatever life throws your way.

What small steps or actions can you take to "dip your toes in" and take those first steps out of your comfort zone?

Start Small

You don't need to take a huge risk or try something you've never done before. You can start with small steps. Here are a few ideas:

1. Strike up a conversation with the person checking you out at the chiropractor's (or dentist's or doctor's) office.

2. Take a different route to work for a change of scenery.

3. Try a new restaurant you've always been intrigued

by, preferably in a part of town you rarely visit, or try an ethnic cuisine you've never sampled.

4. Consider a book by an unfamiliar author or in a genre you would not normally read.

5. Drive down to the basketball or pickleball court and play a game with people you don't know.

....

**The risk of not getting out of your
comfort zone is called regret.**

....

Go Bigger

Once you've made a few forays outside your comfort zone, you'll have the confidence needed to take bigger steps, such as:

1. Find a part-time job. My friend Becki took a part-time job as a bartender at a local bar. She'd never bartended before so naturally felt nervous and scared, but she learned quickly. "If you don't create a comfort zone in the first place, you don't have to step out of it. Be daring, brave, intense, and comfortable being uncomfortable," Becki said. I couldn't have said it any better, and I'm proud of you, Becki!

2. Expand your friendship group. Open the door to

new relationships. My husband and I have friends who do a blind wine tasting in their neighborhood each year. Over the years, it became a popular event, but they created a particularly interesting rule: Only the winner and loser could come back the following year. This allowed new couples or individuals to attend each year. It was important to them to meet new people, and this was one way they could expand their social circle.

3. Try something new. One year for my birthday, my daughter enrolled me in a pottery class, something I hadn't done before. I fretted about my lack of skills, but we both attended class together, and it proved to be a fun night. Even as I botched my one attempt to craft a pottery bowl, I felt as glamourous and adventurous as Demi Moore in *Ghost*. If you haven't seen the movie before, it's said to be the most famous pottery scene in cinema history (go to YouTube to check it out). Although I wasn't the best potter that night, it felt invigorating to get my hands dirty—and I was honoring my commitment to try new things.

4. If you have a phobia, what's something you could do to overcome it one time in a safe environment? For instance, if you fear heights, could you go up

in a tall building and look out the window with a friend?

Continue developing a growth mindset. The most successful people in the world have a deep need for growth that pushes them to leave their comfort zone in search of new opportunities. Developing this muscle will help you unlock your inner compass and help find your true purpose.

Develop a Just "Do It" State of Mind

Like many, I suffered from the old "IDIW" syndrome: "I'll do it when . . . "

- My children are older.
- I have enough money.
- I retire from my day job.
- I lose a few pounds.

Have you done your "it" yet? If your answer is no, I challenge you to get rid of the "I" and "W" on either end of the "IDIW" syndrome. That leaves you with "do it," so just do it!

Why? Before you know it, life will have passed you by. If you don't start now, you won't be able to accomplish as much as I know you can, as much as you want. So the next time you're faced with a challenge or there's something you've always dreamed of doing, say these two magic words aloud: "do it." Then step out and experience the thrill as you start tackling tasks you never thought you could.

What you're really saying is: "I believe in myself. I value myself. I honor my true desires. I believe I can do this. I am doing this."

My youngest daughter, Kaitlyn, played on the varsity softball team in high school. During one of the games in the latter part of the season, she was up to bat in the bottom of the last inning, bases loaded, two outs, with the score tied. The outcome would determine the team's seed in the Division 1 playoffs, a steppingstone to the State Championships.

Undone by the stress, I hid behind the bleachers where I didn't have to watch but could hear the umpire call the next six pitches. Kaitlyn fouled off the first two pitches, and then the pitcher threw three balls in a row. *Three balls and two strikes.*

To my great delight, I then heard the crack of the bat and the home crowd fans clapping and cheering. I rounded the bleachers, just as the ball dropped in shallow right field, and the girl on third ran home. Kaitlyn had made the game-winning hit.

After the game, I asked Kaitlyn what she was thinking at the plate, knowing the game rested on her shoulders. She looked me in the eye and said, "I just had to do it. There was no other choice. I just had to do it." Look at what she accomplished when she believed in herself.

A few years earlier, my oldest daughter was a freshman on the cross-country team. Daralyn's leg had been hurting during practices for a couple of weeks, but we didn't think too much of it. As you might suspect, her next Saturday morning meet did not end well. We all knew something was wrong when all the other runners had crossed the finish line and she was nowhere to be seen. At last, we could see her far off in the distance, running/hopping toward the finish line. Her dad ran toward her to see what was wrong, but she stayed focused on the finish line. Once there, Daralyn collapsed, and her dad picked her up and drove her to the emergency room.

At the emergency room, as they were putting her bright pink cast on, I asked Daralyn why she chose to finish the race, when it would have been easier to lie down until help arrived. "I never quit a race," she said, "I'm not a quitter." Even when injured, she honored her commitment to herself. She embodied that "do it" mentality, but neither she nor I would recommend that anyone run on a broken leg—ever.

. . . .

"Do it"—what if you lived by those two
little words? Stop holding yourself back and decide
to *do it*. If you've always wanted to start a side
hustle, run a 5K, or open a small bakery because
baking is your passion, go for it. Be courageous and
honor yourself; commitment will follow.

. . . .

Claim Your Superpowers

You are more badass than you imagine yourself to be. Few get to be adults without going through tough challenges. It is common for people to experience feelings of worry, fear, or even embarrassment whenever there is a disruption in life. It's possible that this time in your life is one of those moments that completely takes you by surprise or knocks you for a loop. But when it's over and enough time has passed for you to be able to reflect on the experience, you may see it from a different perspective. You may see more clearly how you did overcome those trying moments or what you could have done differently. Reflection allows you to realize you possess real-life superpowers.

What are superpowers? Superpowers are the personal assets you've amassed, based on experiences you've lived through. These might include endurance, resilience, empathy, independence, perseverance, humility, determination, and grit.

I have a dear friend who had a baby when she was fourteen. Taking care of an infant while also attending school was just one of the many challenges she had to overcome. She showed tremendous perseverance and muddled through the hardest years. Today, she is using the skills she developed all those years ago to become a successful business owner as well as an incredible human being.

From my perspective, growing up in a dysfunctional home and dealing with the sense of instability it created provided me with my superpower of resiliency, which has come in handy many times throughout my life.

We all have unique superpowers that develop as we overcome obstacles and learn from our experiences. Our superpowers will help us get through the most challenging times. Be proud of your superpowers; they set you apart and make you unique and awesome at the same time.

Create Your "Courage Catalog"

To bolster your list of superpowers, think back on all the times you felt a deep sense of accomplishment in your life. It can be anything that makes you feel proud of yourself. Once you create this list, it will be something you can lean on in times of doubt, when you need a boost of courage to overcome fear. This is your "Courage Catalog."

Questions to help you think about the courageous times in your life include:

1. Have you ever started a successful side hustle? Write a paragraph about what you did to make it successful.

2. Did you go back to school and earn a degree? What were the circumstances, and what obstacles did you overcome?

3. Have you ever given a presentation that earned rave reviews? How did you make that happen?

4. Think about a project in which your efforts exceeded expectations. It could be a project you completed at home, as a volunteer, or at church. What skills did you showcase during the project?

5. Have you ever learned a new skill? What was it, and what steps did you take to learn this new skill?

6. Have you ever experienced a breakup or some heartache and made it through? How did you make it through? Write a paragraph about the experience.

7. Have you ever run a distance race (5k, 10k, half marathon, or marathon)? If so, how did you prepare for it?

8. Have you gone through a difficult divorce and are succeeding on your own now? Explain your independence journey.

9. Have you ever had to deal with a setback? How did you address it?

10. Have you ever tried something that scared you? What was it, and how did you fight past your fear?

These are sample questions. If needed, produce your own questions based on your personal experiences. The whole point is for you to see that you've been through a lot in your life. You've overcome fear, obstacles, heartbreaks, and roadblocks, and even if they now feel less daunting, these were major accomplishments that required courage.

Pick your top three proudest moments and relive them in your mind—over and over—until they are fully integrated into your being. This is how your "courage catalog" will become your real-life confidence booster. By recognizing your superpowers and creating a courage catalog, you're on your way to being a courageous person who honors her commitments to herself and others.

Closing Notes

Faith over fear. Start the side hustle. Read a new genre. Try an ethnic restaurant. Climb a mountain. Make the call. Introduce yourself. Inquire. Try a new hobby. Sign up for the 5k. Go sky diving. Try yoga. Learn how to take videos. Podcast it. Book it. Cook it. Bake it. Hire the coach. Take the vacation. Be a good human being. Don't give in to fear.

Face Your Fears Exercises

What will it take for you to leave your comfort zone?

- Either in your journal or the space below, write down two actions you will take in the next thirty days that will require leaving your comfort zone. Once you've completed your two comfort zone busters, go back to your journal and record how you felt after putting yourself out there. Did you feel exhilarated after taking a new class, or did you find it tedious? You get the picture.

_____

_____

_____

_____

- Try the risk/result exercise. Write down past risks you have taken and their results. Try to think of at least three examples. Here's an example from my life: **Risk**: I joined the USMC at eighteen, without discussing it with my parents. No one in my family had ever been in the military. I had never even been on a plane. **Result**: I learned that I was courageous; I discovered new skills; I developed discipline and focus; I traveled the world; I met my ex-husband and had two beautiful daughters. I lived in Okinawa, Japan, Hawaii, California, and North Carolina. Surprisingly good results from one risk, wouldn't you say? Now it's your turn.

- What personal stories showcase *your* superpowers? Write them down as a way to recognize and honor what you've been through, what you learned to survive, and what you've accomplished. Give yourself bonus points for having the commitment, courage, and honor to face down your fears and overcome your challenges.

- Create a "Courage Catalog" of your own.

Principle #5: Create Your Bucket List

EAGLE

Description: No other bird soars higher than an eagle. Foster your eagle energy by seeking adventure. Fly high and dream big.

Mantras:

I am excited about creating my bucket list.

I deserve to go on adventures that bring me joy.

I will invest more in experiences and less in material possessions.

I commit to cultivating a light, playful, joyful approach to life by living adventurously.

Inspirational Song: "Lush Life," by Zara Larsson. Live a full life by living each day as if it were your last. Create your bucket list today and get busy living that lush life you so richly deserve.

Opening Notes

Do you have a bucket list of the experiences you crave, the places you'd like to visit, events, milestones, or achievements that you hope to have or accomplish during your lifetime? A bucket list is an itemized list of goals to accomplish before you "kick the bucket."

The term "bucket list" was popularized by a 2007 movie starring Jack Nicholson and Morgan Freeman, in which the two terminally ill characters embarked on a road trip together to complete their life's *wish lists*, vowing to fulfill each desire before they "kicked the bucket."

I often hear people say: "I've always wanted to sky dive, travel to Europe, or run a half marathon." Few ever do. Most spend their lives hoping that their hectic schedule will eventually ease, at which point they'll finally get around to doing everything they've been putting off. It's normal to put off living one's dreams until the "perfect" moment arrives. Unfortunately, for some people the "perfect time" never comes.

To build a plan for the rest of your life and to set goals to do the things you've only dreamed about doing, you need a bucket list. Simply creating the list will inspire you to start checking items off, and soon you'll be living life to the fullest.

Creating a bucket list has many feel-good benefits. First, it's exciting to envision doing something you've only vaguely thought about doing. Focusing on what it is and how you'll do it creates buzz, focus, energy, and motivation. Not only does making a bucket list help you abandon your comfort zone, it:

- Provides a sense of accomplishment as items are checked off.

- Serves as a reminder of what's most important to you.

- Helps you experience more joy.

- Motivates you to stay active.

- Helps you have the courage to live your best life.

- Gives you a sense of purpose.

- Serves as a great boredom buster.

- Creates new and lasting memories.

- Gives you something to look forward to.

- Powers up and ignites your inner compass (because you'll be doing things that you've only dreamed about).

> *"Twenty years from now you will be more disappointed by the things that you didn't do than by the ones you did do. So throw off the bowlines. Sail away from the safe harbor. Catch the trade winds in your sails Explore. Dream. Discover."*
>
> —**Mark Twain, author**

Creating a bucket list forces you to look at your life and what you've accomplished versus what you desire to do. Life is about experiences, and a bucket list can provide amazing experiences that give you a sense of pride and accomplishment. Your bucket list should be meaningful and personal to you. It's your chance to dream big, so jot down everything you've ever wanted to see, do, feel, and experience. Release all inhibitions and don't be afraid to write anything and everything down. You can always trim it back.

If you're not comfortable calling it a "bucket list," consider another title, such as: "My Adventures" list, my "Nailed It" list, or my "Dream It, Do It" list. Choose whatever title motivates you to think hard and dream big.

It may be beneficial for you to do a self-inventory when considering ideas for your bucket list. Completing the following open-ended questions will assist you in organizing your ideas and getting that bucket list down on paper:

- Are there any interests you would like to pursue?

- What activities make you happy?

- Is there something you would like to learn how to do?

- Is there something you would like to experience or see?

- If money were no object, what would you do right now?

TIP: Your bucket list should be a living record. Examine it frequently and adjust, as necessary. Consider your bucket list a frequently referenced *to-do* list. As you complete items on your bucket list, relish the tremendous sense of accomplishment you'll feel. The most important tip of all: Check items off your list!

How to Create a Bucket List

Instead of waiting until you are close to retirement, sick, or near death, make a bucket list now. Do it while you are healthy and full of life. If you're unsure where to start or how to make one, follow these four simple steps.

1. Name your bucket list. It can be "My Bucket List" or any other name you choose.

2. Decide what kind of bucket list you want. Do

you want an all-encompassing list or a list for the next year? Do you want to choose to do activities or experiences before a certain age, like "Forty Bucket List Items to Do Before I turn Forty," or do you want a seasonal list like "My Summer Bucket List"? You could even create categories, such as "My Relationship Bucket List." You may want a "Travel Bucket List." As you can see, it can be whatever you want it to be.

3. Brainstorm ideas for your list. I'm sure you already have thoughts and ideas, but you will get stuck at some point. When you get stuck, below are additional resources you can check out for inspiration:

   a. *Bucketlist.net*—You can get ideas and create an electronic list of ideas. The top five bucket list ideas on this site include:
      1. See the Northern Lights.
      2. Skydive.
      3. Get a Tattoo.
      4. Go on a Cruise.
      5. Swim with Dolphins.

   b. *I Wish* App—This app has plenty of ideas (over 1200) to help you achieve your bucket list dreams, and you can access it from your phone.

c. *Visited: My Travel World Map*—This app has over 8,000 reviews at the time of this writing. Track your experiences around the world as you tick places off your travel bucket list.

d. Go to Pinterest or Google and type in "bucket list" for additional ideas.

TIP: Before you download any bucket list app, look for these basic features:

Security: The most important feature of any app you download to a smart device is security. Make sure the app protects your personal information.

Timelines: Will having the ability to add a timeline or deadline help you achieve your bucket list adventure? If so, then look for this feature.

Social and sharing capabilities: Do you want the ability to add contacts or friends? This is a great idea if you would like to collaborate on your list with other people. Do you want to be able to share your list on social media?

Reviews: Lastly, make sure your bucket list app has reviews and read them. Not all apps are created equal.

4. Play "ten questions" (or as many questions as possible) with friends. Here are some questions to get you started:

   a. What are places you've only dreamed of visiting?

   b. What sporting event would you like to see in person?

   c. If you had a genie in a bottle, what three wishes would you ask for?

   d. I don't want to regret not doing _____ (respond to this question more than once).

   e. What was one of your childhood dreams?

   f. If you only had one year left to live, what is the one thing you would want to do?

   g. Is there an experience you've always wanted to try close to home?

   h. Is there someone famous you would love to meet?

   i. What's one crazy thing you would love to do, even if it's way out of your comfort zone?

   j. Is there someone you'd like to reconnect with or apologize to before you die?

Regularly update your bucket list. Just think how much fun it will be to check items off, or even to simply review your list and daydream (visualize future adventures). Have fun, be adventurous, and live your best life.

Most importantly, keep yourself accountable. Creating your bucket list is just one aspect of the overall picture. You have to make sure you actually check items off your list. You won't always feel motivated or inspired to complete your bucket list, so you must take measures to ensure you are always pushing forward. How do you do that?

The easiest way to keep yourself accountable is straightforward: talk about it. Tell loved ones about your bucket list. If you created a digital list, share it with a trusted friend.

When you share your bucket list intentions with others, you are starting the manifesting process (more on this in Principle #8). On paper, your bucket list objectives may not seem real. They transform into real-life plans the moment you start saying them out loud.

Creating your bucket list is another way to honor yourself. Once you create the list, stay committed to fulfilling your dreams. By combining honor with commitment, you'll have the courage you need to stay with the just "do it" mindset you learned about in Principle #4.

Wacky Bucket List Ideas

Bucket lists can be grand, but they can also be funny, or

even slightly stange. Here are a few that could fall under this category:

- Dance or kiss in the pouring rain.
- Learn how to pick a lock.
- Be silent for three days.
- Crash a wedding.
- Herd cows.
- Make someone who rarely smiles laugh out loud.
- Shear a sheep.
- Stomp grapes in an Italian vineyard.

I recently asked an on-line forum of retired women from all over the world what they would put on their bucket list. They wanted to:

- Go white water rafting.
- Fly first class.
- Go sand-boarding on the Colorado dunes.
- Live abroad.
- Go up in a hot-air balloon.
- Take a chocolate class in France.
- Go to the Australian Open.
- Help deliver a baby.
- Go dog sledding.

- Visit all the National Parks.
- Play golf in every state.
- Attend a month-long yoga retreat in India.
- Start a fire with a bow drill.
- Learn how to play an instrument.
- Learn to speak a new language.
- Go to the Kentucky Derby and wear a big hat.
- See the bison at Yellowstone National Park.
- Extract honey from a beehive.
- Watch a caterpillar turn into a butterfly.
- Save a life.

When I created a Fall Bucket List for my husband and me one year, I printed it out, framed it, and hung it in a place we could see each day. When we didn't have plans for a weekend, we'd choose something on the list. We completed most activities including:

- Run a 5k.
- Volunteer at a food bank.
- Take a fall hike or bike ride.
- Have a backyard fire.
- Jump in a pile of leaves and take fun pics.
- Visit a pumpkin patch.

- Go for a drive and see the fall leaves.

- Carve pumpkins.

- Bake a fall treat.

- Mix a cozy fall cocktail.

- Cozy up and read a good book.

- Enjoy a German Village Day.

I now do this each season and keep copies of my lists in a notebook so we can revisit memories. You can also write notes on the back to annotate the dates and places you visited or write down the recipe of what you made.

Having a bucket list allows you to both nurture your inner child and live a life filled with hopes, aspirations, excitement, and unlimited possibilities. It serves as a reminder to embrace life's adventures and can have numerous benefits that extend far beyond just checking off items on a list. So take some time to daydream, reflect, and create your bucket list. Let it serve as a catalyst for an extraordinary and fulfilling life.

Closing Notes

Take the trip. Value experiences more than material possessions. Book the flight. Invest in making memories. Go Sailing. Do it now. Be adventurous. Milk a cow. Have fun. Create a bucket list. Be an extra in a movie. Don't wait. Your time here has an expiration date. Life is unpredictable. Here to-

day, gone tomorrow. Live your best life. The possibilities are endless. Be a bucket list buster. Watch a caterpillar turn into a butterfly.

Create Your Bucket List Exercises

Retrieve your journal and do the following:

- Think about the type of bucket list you want to have.

- Name your bucket list.

- Brainstorm ideas for your list and write them all down. Edit later . . . much later.

- Go out with friends and play "ten questions." Remember to bring your journal!

- Get out there and live, live, live.

- Regularly update your bucket list.

- Talk about one of the adventures on your bucket list with a friend or family member this week. Who did you tell? _____

- For fun, in the blank space below, draw a picture of one of your bucket list items.

Principle #6:
Be a Goal Setter

CHAMELEON

Description: Chameleons are masters of change. They change to adapt to their environment, or to keep themselves safe. One of the best ways you can make changes that will improve your life is to set goals.

Mantras:

I am a success waiting to happen.

I have the courage to face anything that comes my way.

I will honor my commitments to myself.

I am laser focused on my goals and committed to going forward.

Inspirational Song: "Girl on Fire," by Alicia Keys. Envision yourself as a "girl on fire" who never backs down from a challenge, who sets goals that scare her. As you set your goals, pretend Alicia Keys is singing this song to *you* and let it truly seep in that "you've got this."

Opening Notes

Every time I strolled down the corridor of the government building I dedicated more than two decades of my life to, I couldn't help but notice the portraits of past leaders adorning the walls. There were very few women on those walls. But instead of feeling disheartened, I harnessed that observation as a catalyst for my own motivation. It served as a constant reminder that we possess the power to set hard goals, smash through barriers, and shatter glass ceilings.

We all need an action plan to get us from point A to point B. Goals provide a framework for achieving everything you want in life. Goals give you a sense of direction and purpose, motivate and inspire you, and put you in the driver's seat of your future. Goal setting allows you to identify what is important in your life and to turn those thoughts and ideas into specific, actionable, and measurable steps. Setting concrete goals is making a commitment to yourself that you will courageously honor. In honoring your commitments, you honor yourself and what truly matters to you.

One of the primary reasons we fail to meet goals is we doubt our abilities. How many times have you thought:

- I want that marketing promotion, but I don't think I have enough experience.

- I want to coach little league soccer, but I don't know all the rules.

- I want to run a 5k, but I'm overweight.

- I'm scared to try it. I'm afraid I'll fail.

Often, we sabotage ourselves without realizing it. Maybe the goal in your head is to get out of debt, yet Amazon packages still show up daily. You want to eat healthier, but you still stock your pantry with chips, chocolates, and sugary cereals.

Maybe you get sidetracked easily. You thought you would have no problem achieving your goal, but you keep letting small stuff get in the way of progress. You might spend too much time on social media in the mornings when you could have used that time to head to the gym. Or you let a little hiccup derail you and allow the negative self-talk to reign.

The best way to reframe your mindset and get from "I can't" to "I can" is by committing your goals to paper.

In December 2022, U.S.C. quarterback Caleb Williams's heartwarming Heisman Trophy Award speech revealed that early setbacks lit a fire inside him. "If you're willing to put in the work and surround yourself with positive people, you can achieve anything," he said. Williams even revealed that he wrote down his goals in a journal. "What used to just be words on a piece of paper has me standing here today."[10]

Goals aren't just for athletes or top executives; goals are for everyone. I'm certain that most successful people created a written list of goals that served as motivation and focus for the careers they forged.

Do you have a dream? If you want to achieve that dream, let's talk goals.

Ground Rules for Goal Setting

Before we discuss methods for setting specific goals, let's begin our discussion by setting parameters for goal creation. Here are basics when it comes to goal setting:

- Goals should be written down. Writing goals down on paper has been shown to bolster commitment. Write it down, make it happen.

- Goals should be challenging yet realistic. Easy goals may not sufficiently motivate you, but unreachable goals may well defeat your purpose. Stretch goals beyond your comfort zone, but keep them within reach.

- Goals should be personal, positive, and written in the present tense.

- Goals should be shared with someone who will help with accountability. This person should be someone who can help you attain your goals by be-lieving in you, lifting you, and genuinely wanting you to become your best self.

- Goals should have flexibility to allow for revision for things out of your control.

- Goals should be based on your values. If you remain unsure of your values, see Principle #3.

- Once a goal is set, maintain unwavering faith in your ability to achieve it.

. . . .

**Most of the barriers you think you are
facing exist solely in your imagination.
Self-doubt is your worst enemy. When creating
or working toward your goals, focus on
positive thoughts.**

. . . .

Brainstorm Your Goals

To set goals, brainstorm a list of what you most want to achieve and then write each goal idea down on paper. For each goal idea, also write why you want to achieve this goal. If you can't answer why, remove it from your list. Write at least two or three solid, valid reasons why this goal matters. Don't skip this step. When you are on the brink of giving up, these whys will get you back on track and committed.

If you are having problems producing a list of goals, first list what you don't want in life. Then, try writing the exact opposite as your goal. This can spark ideas and help you refine your goal.

For instance, if you're tired of feeling broke, the opposite could be: "I want to earn extra income." Now you have a general goal idea that you can further develop later.

TIP: Google is your friend. Need goal inspiration? Go to Google and type in "finance goals" or "health goals." Use whatever pops up for inspiration or to refine your goals.

Identify the Big Ideas

Look at your list of possible goal ideas and circle the big ideas. Big ideas will scare you the most but also excite you at the same time. I like to call these your "chameleon" goals, as they will require real change. The remaining items can be your habits or routines to start. For example, if making the bed each morning is something on your list, this would not be a chameleon goal but more of a routine or habit you'd like to accomplish each morning. If you want to do something you've never done before—such as author a book, run a marathon, or master a new language—these would be considered chameleon goals.

Chameleon goals are generally longer term and have a level of difficulty associated with them, whereas starting a new habit can begin immediately and provide immediate success. We'll discuss more about this later. If you combine productive habits with concrete chameleon goals, your chance of success increases exponentially.

Now, let's discuss a proven method for specific goal setting.

SMART as HELL Goals Defined

George Doran presented the concept of SMART goals in a 1981 Temple University article, "There's a S.M.A.R.T. Way to Write Management Goals and Objectives."[11] Doran's original definition tied to the five letters was Specific, Measurable, Assignable, Realistic, and Time-Related.

To drive a few additional points home, I added HELL to the SMART goals methodology. HELL goals are **H**ard, can be **E**nvisioned, require you to **L**earn a new skill, and **L**eave your comfort zone. Let's go through each SMART as HELL letter and discuss how each applies to setting goals.

Specific: Your written goal should be a detailed statement that specifies what you want to accomplish (think about who, what, where, when, why, and which). For instance, instead of writing "I want a bigger house," write: "I want a 2,500 square-foot, two-story, four-bed-room home with hardwood floors and a home office. I want the home located on a quiet, tree-lined street on the southwest side of town, with a large backyard."

Measurable: Your written goal should say how you will evaluate when and if you met your goal. Use deadlines and numbers to better chart your progress.

Attainable: All goals should be achievable through hard work and dedication. Before committing, ask yourself if it is within your ability to achieve that particular goal, or if you need to revise it. If your goal is to run a 5k, showing up to a race next week with no prior training will likely result in injuries and defeat. Selecting an event several months out and choosing a training plan would be a more reasonable place to start. You also want to consider if you have all the necessary resources.

Relevant/Reason: It's important to specify your compelling reason and motivation for achieving each goal. Is the goal you are chasing worthwhile to you? Does it enhance your life in any way? Why are you doing it? This goal should be personal to you and only you. It should be an exciting goal, fit into your life, and be aligned with your values.

Time Bound: Always set realistic target dates or specific time limits for completion of your goal. Short timelines may make you more productive (but tire you out), while long timelines may allow procrastination. Take time to consider a realistic time period that will push you to work hard but allow for success.

Hard: Your goal should offer a challenge and excite you! Don't make your goals easy to attain. Your goal should lure you outside your comfort zone. Having a hard goal will bring out your best efforts.

Envision: It helps if achieving the goal is something you can envision. We'll talk about specific envisioning techniques later, but basically, being able to see yourself successfully achieving your goal will bolster your ability to succeed.

Learn: Consider any new skills you might learn and make them part of your intention. Learning is always a desirable goal, and it often serves as motivation to set and work toward your goal objectives every day. Dedication, discipline, and determination are key components.

Leave: Each goal is an opportunity to stretch yourself beyond your current comfort zone. This allows growth to happen. Leaving your comfort zone is crucial.

Now, using the principles above, take all the time you need to expand and revise your goal ideas. Once you have them listed, move on to the next task.

Categorize and Prioritize

Now let's review your goal ideas and put them into

categories. Here's a suggested list to get you started:

- Career or Retirement
- Self-Development
- Family
- Finance
- Health
- Fun/Recreation
- Friends
- Spirit/Community

If these don't fit, create your own categories. For instance, if you want to start a romantic relationship, that might be one of your categories. Create whatever works best for you. Once you've broken down your goals into categories, you may need to rank and prioritize them, as you only have so many hours in a day. You can look at them in terms of the next three years, twelve months, or ninety days.

TIP: If long-term goals seem overwhelming, begin by setting small goals for each day. This allows success to breed success. Soon you'll be setting goals for weeks, then months, then a year.

Create an Action Plan

Each major goal you set will likely require a map of the necessary tasks and steps and a detailed schedule for achieving key milestones. Once you create an action list, order them, and identify any needed resources. Devise a strategy to overcome any obstacles that could pop

"The secret of getting ahead is getting started. The secret to getting started is breaking your complex overwhelming tasks into small manageable tasks and then starting on the first one."
—Mark Twain, author

up (excuse buster). You may also need to break action steps down even smaller to make it easier to measure progress.

For a 5k goal, an action plan might look like this:

- I will walk/run for one mile on Mondays, Wednesdays, and Saturdays, starting next Monday.

- In week two, I will walk for one minute and then run for one minute. Excuse buster: If I can't run yet, I will walk three times this week instead of running.

- Or, for this example, I will go to the App store and

download and follow the "Couch to 5K" training program for eight weeks.

- I will strength train every Tuesday and Thursday for thirty minutes.

Resources Needed:

- I will download a 5k training app and follow it.

- I will buy new running shoes.

Obstacles: Write down your excuse busters. These are known as your what/then scenarios.

- What if it's raining outside? Then I will run on the treadmill at the gym.

- What if a work event pops up on a training day? Then I will run on a different day.

- What if I get an injury? Then I will adjust my timeline and push my goal out further, but I will not quit. I will be resilient and persevere despite setbacks, a killer skill in my arsenal.

What will my life look like if I achieve my goal? I will feel better about myself. I will be able to play with my kids without getting winded. I will feel more confident.

Progress Notes: If you ended up with an injury in your 5k training plan, now is the time to adjust strategy. Failure is not an option, but adjusting your goals is more than okay.

Reward: When you accomplish your goal of running your first 5k, then absolutely reward yourself. Maybe an unintended result of training for the 5k enabled you to lose five pounds. Treat yourself to a new outfit or get a massage. Do something nice for you. It's not only much deserved, it reinforces the process of setting and then meeting goals.

Is my Goal SMART as HELL?

- Hard—Is my goal challenging?
- Envisioned—Can I see it clearly in my mind's eye?
- Learn—Am I'm learning a new skill?
- Leave—Am I'm leaving my comfort zone?

Note that you can check these off at the top of the SMART as HELL worksheet.

My SMART as HELL Goal Worksheet

☐ Hard   ☐ Envision   ☐ Learning   ☐ Leaving

COMMITMENT, COURAGE, HONOR

Stated Goal (Specific, Measurable, Time Bound)

S M T

Purpose (Reason)   Start Date: _____

R

Action Plan/Steps with dates

A

What tools do you need to make this happen?

RESOURCES
NEEDED

Excuse Busters (What/Then Scenarios)

OBSTACLES

TAMARASOLT.COM

SMART as HELL worksheet

Keep Track of your progress

PROGRESS
LOG

What my life will look
like when I
achieve my goal

ADDITIONAL
ACTION
STEPS/NOTES

My personal mantra
for achieving my goal

A SMART as HELL goal should be....
challenging , a learning experience, out of your comfort
zone, and something you can envision achieving

TAMARASOLT.COM

NOTE: Go to my website at www.tamarasolt.com
to get access to this form.

Goal Types

There are two types of goals: routine and Chameleon SMART as HELL. Routine goals are those that involve changing habits. To keep these routine goals from absorbing all your focus, I've created a worksheet that will help track routine goals and how you're doing on making the desired changes. You don't need to create SMART as HELL goals for these sorts of daily or weekly routine goals, but tracking them daily really boosts your ability to achieve them. Here's an example I used to get in the habit of making my bed daily:

Routine Goal: Make the bed each morning before coming downstairs.

Start Date: 10-14-2022

Frequency of Routine: Daily

Here's the tracker I developed to keep track of my progress (remember you can request access to this form on my website at www.tamarasolt.com):

ROUTINE/HABIT TRACKER

ROUTINE/HABIT   START DATE _____FREQUENCY_____

1	2	3	4	5	6	7	8	9	10	11
12	13	14	15	16	17	18	19	20	21	22
23	24	25	26	27	28	29	30	31		

1	2	3	4	5	6	7	8	9	10	11
12	13	14	15	16	17	18	19	20	21	22
23	24	25	26	27	28	29	30	31		

COMMITMENT,
COURAGE, HONOR

WHY MAKE THIS A
HABIT?

STEPS REQUIRED TO
MAKE THIS HABIT
STICK

COMPLETION DATE
AND REWARD FOR
ACHIEVING HABIT

NOTES (USE BACK
FOR ADDITIONAL
TRACKING NOTES)

TAMARASOLT.COM

My *Why* for this Routine/Habit

1. It starts my day off in an orderly fashion and thereby helps me approach other tasks with a similar focus.

2. I love the way the smoothed sheets feel when I go to bed each night.

3. My room looks nice when I walk into it, which makes me happy.

Steps to Make My New Routine/Habit Stick

1. Put a yellow sticky on bathroom counter as a reminder.

2. If I forget, make the bed as soon as I think about it.

3. Create a reward for sticking to the routine. For example: If I stick to my goal for ninety days, I can hire a housecleaner or purchase a new bedding set.

Check-in with your routine goals weekly to see how you are doing. If you slipped, write why you failed on the back of your Routine Goal sheet, then get back on track. Noticing what got you off track helps you make appropriate adjustments. Don't beat yourself up; get back at it.

Chameleon SMART as HELL Goals

Chameleon goals involve the breaking down of tasks and more long-term strategy and commitment. For example, if I'm a couch potato but my goal is to run a 5k, my SMART as HELL goals worksheet might look like this:

Goal Statement (Specific, Measurable, Timebound): I will run a 5k by June 2023, and prepare by running three times per week, utilizing a 5k training program that I will download to my phone.

Why: I want to get healthier for myself and my children.

Now just add the action plan you created earlier in the chapter, and you now have a rock-solid SMART as HELL goal. Stay committed to these goals to further ignite your inner compass.

Other Goal Setting Methods: Vision Boards

A vision board is a visualization tool that uses a board of any sort to create a collage of words and pictures that represent your goals. It's as easy as flipping through a stack of magazines, choosing pictures, words, or quotes that align with your unique vision of what you want to happen. You can also write or type words for the board.

Nothing is off-limits when it comes to a vision board. If it's something you can easily add to the board, then add it. The important thing to consider is whether it will help you manifest your vision. We'll talk more about manifestation in Principle #8.

You'll still need to brainstorm goal ideas. It will be best if you are clear on what you want. The difference is that you will be searching for pictures, quotes, or other inspirational materials that are visually pleasing to you.

According to Jack Canfield, creator of the *Chicken Soup for the Soul* anthology series, a vision board that you look at every day has several benefits:

1. It activates the creative powers of your subconscious mind to produce ideas and solutions for achieving your goals.

2. It programs your brain to start noticing the available resources in your environment, some of which were always there, but you never noticed them.

3. It works through the law of attraction by magnetizing and attracting the people, resources, and opportunities you need to achieve your goal.[12]

Vision boards provide clear direction for where you want to go. When you create a vision board, there's no mistaking your priorities, which can help you fast track, manifesting what you deeply desire. When you have a big decision to make, your vision board will also remind you of what matters most to you. Vision boards constantly remind you of your intentions and priorities, which will also help shape your thoughts and actions.

In the 1970s, Jack Canfield used a simple, self-created $100,000 bill that he taped to the ceiling above his bed as his vision board. Every morning he glanced at that $100,000 bill and actively visualized the new lifestyle achieving his goal could bring.

After thirty days of intensely visualizing his new lifestyle, Canfield reported that he began having one-hundred-thousand-dollar ideas. Wow! Can you imagine? Within a year of taping that fake bill to his ceiling, Canfield had earned over $90k, which was far more than his previous year's salary (that would be equivalent in purchasing power to almost $505k in today's dollar). That's the power of a vision board.

If you prefer to do this electronically, you can check out these popular apps for inspiration:

1. *Visuapp Vision Board*—Create a vision board or dreams map with vivid photo's that really pop. Start living the way you really want.

2. *Vision Board*—The description for this app states "when you make a Vision Board you send The Universe powerful signals so it can help you manifest your dreams and desires, utilizing the Law Of Attraction." The app has great reviews.

3. *Vision Board Perfectly Happy*—This app sends

daily reminders to look at your vision board to keep your dreams and goals at the forefront of your mind.

Visualization

Paint a vivid picture in your mind of what success looks and feels like; then make time daily to actively visualize successful achievement of your goal. Your mind is powerful enough to help you make what you envision happen if you reinforce those visualizations daily. Now, visualize yourself doing the work required to achieve your goals. Hold that picture in your mind's eye.

Preeminent golfer Tiger Woods is a master of vivid mental imagery. From an early age, his father, Earl, taught Tiger to mentally envision the successful outcome of his swings or putts. He learned to see each successful move as a snapshot he could see in his mind, and then he used the imagery to set up his shots. "All I am doing is putting to the picture," Tiger explained. "When I'm really nervous, I will go back to that and say, 'Come on, Tiger, just putt to the picture."[13] This visualization technique catapulted Tiger Woods to the top of the golf world.

If you don't understand how to visualize each step to reach your goal, concentrate on how you will feel when you reach your goal.

Write a Letter to Your Future Self

You can also write a letter to yourself or write a check with the desired amount to yourself "for services rendered." It's a potent way to say, "I believe in you" or "I have confidence in you."

Jim Carrey and Bruce Lee successfully utilized this method. Jim Carrey told Oprah Winfrey he wrote himself a check for $10 million, for "Acting Services Rendered," which he post-dated for Thanksgiving, 1995, ten years in his future. "I would visualize having directors interested in me and people that I respected saying, 'I like your work,' and I would visualize things coming to me that I wanted . . . and I had nothing at that time, but it just made me feel better," he shared.[14] He actively visualized earning the amount he wrote on the check and, remarkably, earned that $10 million for *Dumb and Dumber* just before Thanksgiving 1995.

Fellow actor Bruce Lee wrote a letter to himself proclaiming his goals:

"My Definite Chief Aim."

"I, Bruce Lee, will be the first highest paid Oriental superstar in the United States. In return, I will give the most exciting performances and render the best quality in the capacity of an actor. Starting in 1970, I will achieve world fame, and from then onward, till the end of 1980, I will have in my possession $10,000,000. I will live the way I please and achieve inner harmony and happiness.

Bruce Lee, Jan. 1969[15]

Unfortunately, Bruce Lee died in 1973, at the youthful age of thirty-two, but not before he achieved all his goals.

> *"What would you attempt to do if you knew you could not fail?"*
>
> **—Robert Schuller, motivational speaker**

Goal Affirmations

Another suggestion for achieving your dreams and goals is using affirmations, coupling positive thinking with self-empowerment. Make your hopes, dreams, and goals come true by speaking (and then acting) as if they are already happening. To do this, add "I am" to the beginning of your goal affirmation statement. Next, add a feeling action word, in the present tense. For example, if my goal is to run a 5k, my goal affirmation would be: "I am successfully running a 5k."

To take it one step further, I suggest doing this exercise with your number one goal: Write this positive affirmation ten times a day in your journal. Write it down, and make it happen.

One of my limiting beliefs was that I was not a writer. Still, I wanted to write a book, so I changed my limiting belief that I was not a writer to: "I am working on my writing skills every single day." I wrote this sentence ten times a day and truly started to believe in myself.

Mind Maps

A mind map is a way to facilitate brainstorming thoughts. It allows you to visually structure your ideas by starting with a central word or concept that you write in the middle of the page and then circle. From that word or phrase, you then write down any thoughts that arise as a branch. You keep creating branches until you have something that resembles a giant spiderweb.

Mind mapping is an activity that is both analytical and artistic at the same time. Mind maps can be used for idea generation, which might include:

- Brainstorming goal ideas
- Problem solving
- Studying and memorization
- Planning
- Sparking your creativity

With the aid of mind mapping, you can transform

a long, dry list of facts into an engaging and easily digestible visual representation that follows the way your brain naturally thinks.

If this sounds like something you'd like to try, get a piece of paper, and in the middle, write GOALS and circle it. Next, create branches for Career, Self-Development, Family, Finance, Health, Fun/Recreation, Friends, and Spirit/Community, and then circle each. You don't have to use these categories, you can create your own.

Next, create smaller branches from the categories above and start brainstorming additional ideas. For example, if one of your career-related goals is to get a new job in a new field, your mind map might include the following:

- Update my resume.

- Attend networking events.

- Create a LinkedIn profile.

- Hire a career coach.

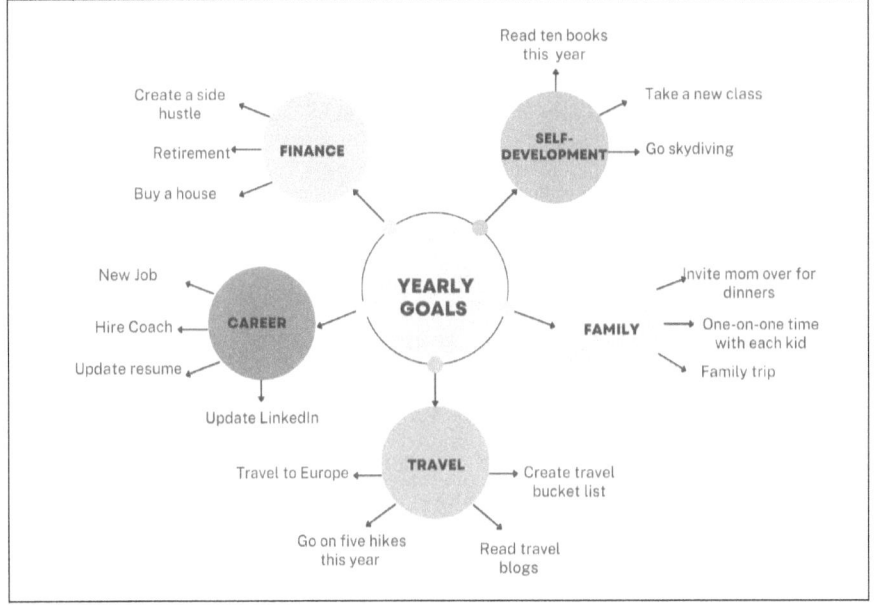

Goal-Setting Mind Map Diagram

Goal Review

Every three to six months, it's helpful to complete an After-Action Review (AAR). The military developed AARs in 1981 to evaluate events in terms of "what I did, why I did it, and how I can improve." The process provided debriefing, reflection, and a way to eliminate excuses, be honest with yourself, and face the person in the mirror.

In his book, *Can't Hurt Me*, David Goggins explained how he used AARs to help him become an accomplished endurance athlete, completing over sixty ultra-marathons and triathlons, setting course records, and regularly placing in the top five.[16]

An AAR includes the following sections:

1. State what you wanted to happen.

2. Acknowledge what actually happened (what went well and what didn't).

3. Write down all the lessons you learned.

4. Adjust and make changes where required to succeed next time.

The AAR is a simple but effective tool to bolster improvement. By regularly assessing your own performance, you'll begin to make small adjustments, which is how growth happens. As you reflect on and learn from your successes and challenges, your motivation and confidence grow.

Overcome Obstacles

Mentally, be prepared for obstacles and possibly a few failures. Failure happens, and it's up to you to be resilient and get back on track. Did you know that Abraham Lincoln struggled mightily with failure before becoming our sixteenth U.S. President in 1861? Remember, it takes courage to fail.

In 1832 he lost his job and his campaign for state legislature.

- In 1833 his business failed.

- In 1835 the woman he loved died.

- In 1836 he had a nervous breakdown.

- In 1838 he lost his chance to become the Illinois House Speaker.

- In 1843 he lost his bid for the U.S. Congress.

- In 1848 he again lost a chance to run for Congress.

- In 1854 he ran, but lost his bid to become Illinois's U.S. Senator.

- In 1856 he sought but did not become the Vice-Presidential candidate.

- In 1858 he lost his second bid for U. S. Senator from Illinois.[17]

Despite all the setbacks, Lincoln persevered, valiantly serving his country with all the lessons learned from his multiple "failures."

No matter what goal you choose, obstacles always arise, and many will seem insurmountable. Be like Lincoln and keep plugging away, rejecting failure, and trying again. When obstacles arise, strategize ways to get around them or through them. You may have to make trade-offs and be willing to pay the costs (a trade-off might be getting up earlier than you normally do to complete a task). Are you willing to accept the sacrifices required to achieve your goals, targets, and objectives? If the answer is yes, ask yourself, "If I succeed, what will my life look like"? Vivid mental images are essential to creating opportunities.

Most successful people are goal-centric and committed. Anything can happen if you write it down, believe it wholeheartedly, and stay focused on your goals. Remember: visualization is key.

Closing Notes

Now go back and listen to the empowering song for this chapter. When you start setting goals and putting in the work to achieve them, you will be on fire! Be proud. Create good habits. Remember where you started and celebrate how far you've come. Forge your own path. Invest in yourself. Believe in yourself. If you fall, get back up. Create hard goals.

Be a Goal Setter Exercises

This is where you'll really peg your goals and write your goal statements:

In your journal or the space provided below, brainstorm goal ideas.

_____

_____

_____

_____

Let's take one of your chameleon goal ideas and create a SMART as HELL goal.

GOAL STATEMENT:

- Specific:

- Measurable:

- Action plan:

- Reason (Why):

- Timebound:

Let's make sure this goal is also **SMART** as **HELL**:

- Is it Hard enough to challenge me?

- Can I Envision the goal? Is it something I can see clearly in my mind's eye?

- Does it require me to Learn a new skill?

- Does it encourage me to Leave my comfort zone?

Use the following techniques to meet your goals:

- Actively visualize your success—this is key!

- Download a vision board app or physically create a vision board for your goals and put it somewhere you will see it daily.

- Write a letter to your future self or post-date a check "for services rendered" and look at it often. Always believe in yourself.

- Make a mind map of goals and the steps needed to achieve them.

- Write goal affirmations and read them regularly.

REMEMBER: Use the tools provided to track your progress. Go to www.tamarasolt.com to access the SMART as HELL Goals worksheet and the Routine/Habit Tracker. Print however many you need and use them to keep track of your progress toward your goals. I use a three-ring binder to keep all these forms in one place.

Principle #7: Try a Side Hustle

BEE

Description: Bees are the one of hardest working insects on the planet, hence a symbol of focus, dedication, resourcefulness, and commitment. Taking on a side hustle can allow you to try new things, have fun, and use your creativity while minimizing financial risk.

Mantras:

Instead of problems, I see opportunities.

I am going to be financially independent.

It's not how you start the race; it's how you finish.

I have the courage to work as hard as required.

Inspirational Song: "She Works Hard for the Money," by Donna Summer. Side hustles can be a game changer, but working a day job and a side hustle requires tremendous commitment, strength, and courage. You will be busy as a bee and need to dig deep for skills such as patience, resourcefulness, and drive.

Opening Notes

Stuck in your current job? Need additional experience? Want extra spending money? Need a change? Want a creative outlet? Taking on a side hustle might be exactly what you need. Side hustles require commitment, courage, and honor to dig deep and stay focused, but it's an excellent way to find your inner compass.

A side hustle is a flexible job that brings in extra money beyond your regular job and main source of income. It's different from a part-time job. With a part-time job, you still have a boss who schedules you and is in charge. With a side hustle, you make your own hours, and you're the boss.

Side hustles come in all shapes and forms. They can be as simple as making cards or signs with a Cricut machine and selling your products to friends and family, or opening a brick-and-mortar business, while keeping your day job. The scope is up to you. Popular side hustles include:

- Selling handmade goods on Etsy.
- Selling used clothing on Poshmark.
- Freelance writing for blogs or magazines.
- Teaching English online.
- Freelance photography.

- Selling vintage pieces through Instagram.

- Lawn care services.

- Dog walking or pet sitting.

- House cleaning.

- Providing a service on Fiverr or Upwork.

- Creating a YouTube channel with subscribers.

- Car detailing.

- Personal training.

- Starting a blog.

- Officiating weddings.

- Teaching a class such as yoga or making hand-made cards.

These are just examples. See what ideas you can produce for yourself.

Top Seven Benefits of Starting a Side Hustle

Working a side hustle allows you to explore other opportunities and interests. The top seven benefits of starting a side hustle are:

1. **It can help you land a new job**. At my last job, I interviewed for a position to supervise a team of ten employees. I had no previous experience as a government supervisor, but I used my experience as a small business owner, noting that

I supervised employees, interviewed new hires, provided feedback, created a training packet, and processed payroll, to name a few. The person who hired me said my side hustle experience gave me the needed edge, and I got the job.

2. **It can uncover a hidden passion.** After discovering my passion for vintage at a live auction, I rented space at an antique mall and also opened an Etsy shop.

3. **It increases financial security.** When my husband and I owned Hop Yard 62, we rarely paid ourselves. Because we both had full-time jobs, we were able to put 100% of any income we did receive into a savings account. From that savings account, we were able to pay down our mortgage and within five years we had paid off our house.

4. **It helps you explore your creativity.** When we owned Hop Yard, I loved designing T-shirts and other unique merchandise. I started a second-chance line of branded clothing. Second-chance pieces were previously owned thrifted items making them one-of-a-kind. I also liked finding unique ways to bring new customers through the door. Sometimes it's hard to be creative at your day job, but with a side hustle, the sky's the limit. My side hustle made me happy.

5. **It adds new skills to your portfolio.** I enjoyed flipping furniture because it allowed me to learn a useful skill. I soon became skilled at painting furniture and upcycling old pieces into something new. I even converted an antique sewing machine cabinet into an upscale bar cart.

6. **It gets you out of your comfort zone and helps you overcome fear.** When I started selling vintage, I had to set up a booth and talk to people. Talking to strangers made me anxious, so I adopted the just "do it" attitude I learned in the Marines and forced myself to engage with potential customers. The more I engaged, the easier it became.

7. **It bolsters ingenuity.** Our "grand-opening night" at Hop Yard was filled to capacity, with people lined up outside to get in. Suddenly our brand-new Point of Sale (POS) system stopped working, meaning we could not process any payments. Initially we panicked. We hadn't planned for this sort of problem to happen. After asking our excited patrons for patience, we called the vendor, who then walked us through the fix. Within thirty minutes, we were finally able to process customer payments. We survived and learned so much that first night.

Creating a side hustle can literally change your life. It can provide financial freedom while simultaneously allowing you to pursue a passion and to assess the market to see if it is viable. It will, however, require commitment at the onset. Whatever you choose to explore, you will encounter obstacles and snags along the way. Don't let that scare you, though. Take it one tiny step at a time, and before you know it, those obstacles will be in the rearview mirror.

Side hustles sometimes require little monetary investment, making it lucrative. A person who wants to make extra cash as a musician or photographer may have long enjoyed the hobby and already have sufficient equipment to get started. A dog sitter may have zero cash outlay, but as long as she loves dogs, she can launch her business. With either of these side hustles, you can name your price and set your own hours. Because you can set your own hours, a person could have multiple side hustles. Doesn't this sound just about perfect?

> **TIP**: Never choose a side hustle that interferes with your day job. First, make sure your company doesn't prohibit such activities, which may be the case if what you do for your day job is similar to what you'll be doing as a side hustle. For instance, if you work for an engineering firm, providing similar services in the evenings on Fiverr.com would not be a smart idea. It could end up getting you fired. Be cautious when choosing your side hustle.

Discover and Implement Your Perfect Side Hustle

Here's some tips I learned when creating my side hustles:

1. **Brainstorm to find ideas that excite you.** Once you have identified ten or so ideas, narrow it down to your top three.

2. **List everything you need to get started.** For instance, if you want to sell clothes on Poshmark, you'll need to study their website to see how you go about setting up your account, as well as what's currently selling. You'll also want to find stories about people who've successfully run a similar business and take advantage of their learning process. On Etsy, you'll need to study potential competition and figure where you'll fit in the market. Other considerations might be whether or not you need business cards, if you need a website, Facebook page, or Instagram account, which supplies you'll need, and where you will find your customers.

3. **Estimate potential costs.** For each of your top three ideas, list everything you'll need to purchase to get started. If one appears to be too costly, go to the next idea. You'll want to trust your inner compass when it comes to which one feels the most

right, which one you can fully commit to pursuing, but always remember that your ultimate goal is to make money, not go into debt.

4. **Talk to people who have started similar side hustles.** Do you have a friend who sells on eBay, Poshmark, Etsy, or through Instagram? If so, reach out and ask how they got started. Most people are willing to share what they've learned. For instance, if you're thinking about starting a personal training business, talk to gym owners to see if they're looking for additional trainers. Find out what certifications you need. Make a commitment to discover as much as you can, do your homework, and be a self-starter.

5. **Keep records.** Once you've settled on an idea and implement it, track all your expenses and your income. Keep accurate records and all receipts in case you later need to hire an accountant.

6. **Review what's working and what's not.** After six months, complete an in-depth After Action Review (AAR) so you can make any needed adjustments. (AARs were discussed in Principle #6.)

7. **Financial Considerations:** Once your side hustle starts generating income, it's essential to consider how you'll utilize those earnings. Will you reinvest

them into furthering your side hustle's growth? Or perhaps allocate them towards covering bills, reducing your mortgage, or even indulging in enjoyable experiences like travel, date nights, or treating yourself to a new bike. The possibilities are endless, and it's up to you to decide how to make the most of your hard-earned money from your thriving side hustle.

···

The three most important skills you will need to start a side hustle are self-motivation, the willingness to learn, and commitment to do the challenging work that will come. If you are reading this book, you more than likely already possess these skills.

···

My Side Hustle Progression

With each side hustle attempt, you will gain valuable, marketable skills that increase your confidence, foster commitment, build your courage, and open a plethora of opportunities. It's another way to honor yourself by acting on this idea that has been steadily percolating inside your subconscious mind.

Let's say you decide to start selling your craft creations on Instagram or Facebook Marketplace. You can sell through your personal page or start a new page with your side hustle name. You make your items, research comparable items on the chosen site to determine what price you'll charge, take high-quality photographs of each item, and then post your products on-line. Just imagine how exhilarating it will feel when someone becomes your first sale. With each sale, your courage and confidence grow. People may begin requesting custom orders. As time goes by, you gain more skills and experience, learn what works and what doesn't, the best times to post, and how to identify your target customer. You progress until business is booming, and you decide it's time to create your own website.

I've had six side hustles in my life so far, and each taught me something new. Each served as a progression. I'll offer examples of my side hustles, in the hope they will inspire you to find your own.

eBay Side Hustle

In the 1990s, selling gently used clothing on eBay looked easy. I knew I could make more money selling kids clothing on eBay than I could at a garage sale or resale shops. Selling on eBay required taking detailed photographs, providing measurements, and research on pricing and how best to stand out, as well as the time it took to upload everything, but I didn't let anything scare me off. Once I got my products in place, if they didn't sell, all I had to do was hit the "relist" button. eBay also messaged your phone a "cha-ching" sound each time you received an offer or made a sale. That sound became music to my ears.

Best of all, selling clothes on eBay gave me transferable skills that would quickly ramp up future side hustles. As an eBay merchant, I learned how to take effective product photos, write engaging product descriptions, Search Engine Optimization (SEO), set up shipping, ship items in the most economical way, and handle customer service requests and complaints.

Team Camo Gear Side Hustle

Team Camo Gear came next. Mixing my love of college sports and camo with my "get it done" Marine spirit, I founded a company to make team-colored camouflage clothing for people who wanted to wear something fun and unique to support their teams at sporting events— or anywhere. I hired a web designer to create a website, through which I marketed the product line. I loved writing the user requirements for the website and creating marketing materials.

My Team Camo Gear side hustle provided the following knowledge, skills, and abilities:

- How to enlist SCORE (Service Corps of Retired Executives) as advisors, which is an outstanding resource for anyone planning to start a business.

To learn more about SCORE, go to https://www.score.org.

- How to write a formal business plan.

- How to hire a web programmer and design the web concept.

- How to secure a vendor's license.

- How to register my business name with the State of Ohio.

- How to create a company logo (I used www.fiverr.com).

- How to register to become a dealer with a camouflage wholesaler.

- How to design business cards.

- How to use Quick Books.

- How to obtain a business bank account and credit card.

- How to sign up for and manage events.

- How to create a Google Ads campaign.

I didn't break the bank with this idea, but what I learned definitely progressed the skillset I'd learned from eBay and prepared me for new business ventures. I ran it for a couple years, but when it stopped being fun, I closed the shop to take a break.

Furniture Flipping Side Hustle

One day I noticed a well-worn dresser on the side of the road and enlisted my husband to help me bring it home. Upon examining it, I discovered it had solid bones and decided I'd paint it and sell it for a profit.

I'd been reading blogs about a new painting method using chalk paint and thought, why not? Using the information I'd learned from the blogs, I bought paint, un-sanded tile grout, and Johnson's paste wax. I mixed the un-sanded tile grout with a little water, then added the paint (a homemade chalk paint recipe to save money) and began painting. Once I was done, I applied the paste wax and let it cure for about a week.

Despite it being my first attempt at refinishing and chalk painting, my creative experiment turned out fantastic. I took photos, listed it on Craigslist for $150, and sold it a few days later. I'd found something I thoroughly enjoyed, with an amazing profit margin. Of course, you won't find free furniture on the side of the road often, but thrift shops often have treasures, as do yard sales. I loved using my hands to restore or transform a previously unloved item and help it avoid the dreaded landfill. I did this for a few years until the market became saturated with other DIYers flipping furniture. With this side hustle I learned:

- How to source items.

- How to keep up with market trends, as it related to painted furniture in the secondary market.

- How to make my own paint to avoid paying $40 a gallon for pre-made chalk paint.

- How to set pricing and handle market saturation.

- How to change out the hardware on a furniture piece, which could make all the difference.

- How discovering what you can do with a little bit of sweat equity is priceless.

Antique Mall Side Hustle

After attending the live auction that provided my "aha moment," I called every antique mall in Columbus, Ohio, to see if anyone had an open booth space. As luck would have it, a small antique mall close to me had a small, starter space open. As soon as I saw it, I rented it—and I only had the few pieces I had won at the auction. To quickly build inventory, I shopped auctions and thrift stores after work.

I rented that small space for almost three years, during which time I also launched an Etsy shop. Because I could sell vintage items on Etsy for a higher profit and make money while I slept, I closed the mall shop and focused on Etsy.

Skills I learned at the antique mall:

- To be choosy. At first, I bought everything vintage or antique I could afford, but I quickly learned not everything sells. I learned to be more selective when I purchased inventory.

- How to artfully display items, which had not been a strength previously.

- How to price vintage items.

- My tastes. In time I discovered that I prefer vintage (anything 20 to 100 years old) over actual antiques (anything over 100 years old).

- How limiting running a shop can be. Having a physical space not only required a lot of sweat equity, it also limited potential sales to six hours a day when the antique mall was open. By switching to an online platform, I could make sales 24/7.

Etsy Side Hustle

I still sell vintage in my Buffalo Plaid Vintage Etsy shop, which can be found at www.etsy.com/shop/Buffalo PlaidVintage, for which I store at least 500 items in my basement, in carefully organized tubs. I frequent thrift shops, yard sales, and estate sales. I've even purchased vintage items on vacation and toted them home on the plane. I've stuck with this one because my passion for vintage remains strong. At the time of this writing, I've had over 1,500 sales on Etsy.

This side hustle doesn't earn enough to pay a mortgage, but I like that I am doing something I love. I love sourcing items; it's the thrill of the hunt. I also love the opportunity to keep something out of the landfill and extend its life. Older pieces are much better made compared to today's throw-away culture, where many pieces are made of cheap particle board or plastic. And, as I said earlier, I like making money while I sleep.

"If you don't find a way to make money while you sleep, you will work until you die."

—Warren Buffet, American business magnate, investor, and philanthropist

My Etsy money did pay a portion of my kids' college, a portion of both daughter's weddings, and allowed us to travel and cross items off my bucket list. That's the true power of a side hustle.

Skills I am still learning while selling on Etsy:

- How an online shop is like a physical shop. It needs to be regularly updated, or it looks stale to customers.

- How to take quality photographs—which are everything when you sell online.

- How to research your products, find out what the competition is selling, and make sure you're not the highest or lowest offering.

- How to provide exceptional customer service.

- How to keep accurate records for the end-of-year tax season.

- How to organize and store inventory. You'll flip out if someone buys a small item that's not in the right container and it takes hours to find it.

Craft Beer and Wine Bar Business

This business was by far the ultimate side hustle for us. When my husband Greg and I imagined it would be both profitable and fun to open a craft beer bar in our small hometown, we started visiting breweries wherever we traveled. In each, we'd make notes about what we liked at the brewery's bar, in case we had an opportunity to cash in on our dream. In hindsight, I don't know what we were thinking since we both had full-time jobs, but for some reason, we were drawn to this idea.

We were regulars at a local gathering place in our hometown, and when it sold in 2015 and soon after went from being packed to almost no customers, wheels started spinning. Could this be our place?

Greg and I had zero experience running a bar, let alone opening a brick-and-mortar business. We had a vision, but was that enough? We decided to ask the original owners, who were also friends, if they would like to partner with us. Without hesitation, they said "Yes," and we put our offer together, submitted it to the real-estate agent, and the rest is history. After spending only five weeks building out the new concept, we opened to an overflow crowd, proving we had something rare and special.

This remains the most rewarding side hustle I've ever had. I still sometimes can't believe that we ran a successful craft beer bar for almost six years, right through the pandemic of 2020. From a sales perspective, we had the best summer we ever had that summer of 2020 because we learned how to pivot quickly. I wouldn't change that experience for anything. I could probably write a entire book about how we did this for almost six years, raised some teenagers, and worked full-time. Hint: hire the right employees and treat them well—end of the story.

Skills I learned while running a craft beer and wine bar included:

- How to apply human resources expertise to source, train, and develop dependable team members.

- How to create a branded, second-chance clothing line with thrifted shirts and sweatshirts (this was a passion project).

- How to create branded T-shirt designs and other logo wear.
- How to capitalize on social media platforms such as Facebook, Instagram, and Untappd to increase market awareness and brand recognition.
- How to create realistic budgets for effectively operating a business.
- How to stay current with market trends to determine the optimal pricing of goods.
- How to establish company culture with exacting standards of cleanliness and customer service.
- How to implement effective marketing and customer engagement plans to build from nothing to a recognized brand in less than three years.
- How to map income-generating strategies to grow revenue.
- How to evaluate the effectiveness of events and promotions.
- How to maintain Point of Sale System for sales, reports, and reconciliation.
- How to perform payroll functions, write extensive Standard Operating Procedures (SOPs), create job descriptions, and perform end-of-year reviews.
- How to create training checklists for new employees.

- How to interview job candidates, schedule employee shifts, and reconcile bank deposits.

- How to create franchise documents for future franchise and expansion plans.

- How to create an exit strategy when you're ready to do something else.

We finally sold Hop Yard 62 in November 2020, which proved a bittersweet moment. My mother-in-law's health was failing, we had a new grandchild on the way, work became a little busier for us, and my husband wanted to pursue his master's degree. All good things must end.

"There will be obstacles. There will be doubters. There will be mistakes. But with hard work, there are no limits."

—Michael Phelps, Olympic champion

TIP: Remember to keep your day job. If your side hustle ends or doesn't work out, you'll still want a paycheck coming in. Don't let fear get in the way, and don't let all the tiny details derail you.

I hope my experiences will encourage you to see the massive benefit of experimenting with side hustles. Not only do you evaluate your passions to see if they have legs, but you can test the waters to see if your interests can support you financially. You may also learn new skills that will make you resume more marketable. As those skills progress and expand, more doors will open for you.

Closing Notes

Nobody will fully appreciate how much time and effort you put into your side hustle. You will work hard. You will shed tears. You will encounter doubt. You will have to dig deep. You may even consider giving up. Never give up until you've given it your all. Be proud of trying and prouder of succeeding. Celebrate the small victories. You've come a long way. Commitment, courage, and honor will fuel your success.

Try a Side Hustle Exercises

Get out your journal and complete the following:

- Write down the areas of your life in which you excel. Is there a task that others constantly ask you to do for them? Maybe you can turn this skill into a side hustle.

- Brainstorm some ideas that excite you. Use the mind map exercise we discussed in the last chapter. Once you have a list of ideas, pick your top three.

- Write down everything you need to get started.

- Write down any costs involved.

- Can you reach out to anyone who has started something similar?

I love reading about ordinary people who started successful side hustles. Here's one of my favorite websites: https://www.cnbc.com/make-it/side-hustles/.

If my stories inspired you, please reach out to me and let me know how they helped. I would love to hear from you. Contact me at www.tamarasolt.com or on Instagram @tamarasoltauthor.

Principle #8: Manifest the Life You Desire

BUTTERFLY

Description: Butterflies complete the ultimate transformation, from an egg to a larva, from a pupa to a winged butterfly. They've become a symbol of renewal, rebirth, and powerful transformation. Be like a butterfly. Transform your life from what it is to what you wish it to be. Manifest your deepest desires.

Mantras:

I am ripe for transformation.

I am a magnet for success.

My dreams will come true.

I will create everything and every possession I desire.

Inspirational Song: "Pretty Girl Magic," by Moonlight Scorpio. If you desire success, know that you can attract the success you most desire. Life is what you make of it . . . it becomes what you think about.

Opening Notes

It's your life and whatever transformation you desire is completely up to you. It doesn't matter where or how you grew up, who your family or friends are, or what type of education you have or don't have. Today, right now, you can begin to change your thoughts and have the life you want.

Manifesting is one of my favorite topics. If you completed all the exercises in the previous chapters, this next part will be a cakewalk. Manifesting is simply using your thoughts, feelings, and beliefs to bring something to physical reality. By having a rock-solid vision of what you want in life and regularly and consistently focusing on that vision, you can attract the life you desire. You are what you think you are, the sum of your daily thoughts. When it comes to manifesting desires, mindset and belief are your superpowers.

*"If you are timid, backward, in a rut and
an underling, it is because of yourself. Blame
not the stars. Blame not society. Blame not the
world. Blame yourself. Again, I say change
gears. Put them in high and begin to move."*

—Claude M. Bristol, author

Manifesting is having a thought enter your mind repeatedly until something comes to fruition. I liken it to Facebook bombarding you with ads. Whether Facebook is listening to your conversations or just tracking you by association, they've found a way to repeatedly show you ads that will likely appeal to your sensibility, designed to inspire you to take immediate action. They use a visual image to put the thought into your head, then make it super-duper easy for you to click a link, and presto, you're on the purchase page. That's sort of what manifesting is all about in simplified terms. Instead of a visual image on your computer screen prompting you to act, the images you're holding in your mind will prompt you to act. What you think about most, you attract. This is known as the Law of Attraction.

How Manifesting Works

The process is simple, and everyone reading this can do it. You have the power to change your life—if you believe you can. Here are the four steps you need to master:

1. **Visualize *exactly* what you want**. Begin by being clear about what you want. I had toyed around with the idea of wanting a lake house on several different occasions. Every time we visited Lake Erie, I got caught up in the excitement of the moment and wanted to live the lake life. I guess

I never really thought about all the little details. Nonetheless, six months ago, a friend sent a listing for a lake home near their little bungalow. We drove up to Lake Erie, loved the house, and put an offer in. While we were waiting to learn if the owner accepted our offer, I started having second thoughts. Was this house truly what I wanted? Would we utilize it enough? We'd only get a handful of months to use it due to cold winters. I had acted hastily and really didn't have a clear vision of what I wanted. Fortunately, our offer was not accepted.

2. **Submit your order to the universe**. Take time to describe what you want, in detail, from a grateful heart, and write it down on paper, as if you already have it. You can also create a vision board, as discussed in Principle #6 (the goal-setting chapter). Once you've committed your desire to paper or visuals, mediate daily and see it as already true.

3. **Believe it with all your heart**. When you believe that you deserve to have your desires, that belief releases creative powers. Your subconscious mind finds ways to make it happen, setting events in motion in a way that will make you scratch your head. If you place an order on Amazon for a yoga mat, you have no doubts that you'll get the mat,

right? Envision your desire arriving and trust that it will come—in its own time. While meditating and envisioning, also listen to your inner compass. If it tells you to take a step forward, listen. When I envisioned writing this book, I had no idea what to do beyond writing down thoughts as they arose. My inner compass told me to "write whatever you can," so I did. I took it one step at a time. When you're always worried about the "how," it shows a lack of faith. Remember when you were a child and you thought Santa Claus was real? That kind of belief/mindset is what is really needed in this step.

4. **Prepare to accept what's headed your way.** Take time when meditating to also *feel genuinely* what it would be like to get what you desire. In your mind, see every vivid detail, in color. Where are you in your mental picture? Who is with you? What are you wearing? What can you see, hear, feel, smell, or taste? Take it all in. Remember how Jack Canfield actively visualized what he would buy when he made $100,000. Those visualizations helped him manifest the money.

I Manifested Without Realizing It

Before we even dreamed of owning a craft beer bar, my husband and I loved visiting breweries. When the dream first surfaced, we'd take photos of breweries that impressed us, discuss where they hit the target and where they could have improved. We didn't take pictures to copy anything. We used them solely to inspire us, to develop a clear mental picture of the kind of place we'd like to own one day. I can honestly report that the Law of Attraction delivered exactly what we had been focusing on. Hop Yard 62 became everything we wanted it to be.

If there's something that fascinates you, something you want to manifest, find ways to immerse yourself in exploring whatever it is and use all of your senses to build your own vision of what it could be like.

Learn to Reframe Negativity

Have you ever had a bad day that started as soon as you woke up? You spill coffee on your shirt or blouse before you leave the house. You rush upstairs to change. You're in a slightly bad mood now. You decide to stop by the coffee shop, but the line is wrapped around the building, and you don't have time to wait. Grrr. You take a left turn toward the freeway and notice traffic on the freeway is moving at a snail's pace. You're going to be late for a 9:00 a.m. meeting with your boss. Now you're in a horrible mood. You wonder if you should turn around and take the day off or, better yet, go back to bed and try starting over.

You may not have known that you began actively manifesting what you were feeling—that initial "slightly bad mood"—moments after the first event. When you become aware of this phenomenon, you can learn to halt those negative feelings right from the get-go.

If you want to change a bad day to a good day, curb that negative mindset and immediately revert to thinking positive thoughts. If you're still struggling to get out of a bad mood, try visualizing something happy or, better yet doing something that makes you happy. Create a "Things that Make Me Smile" list and use it whenever necessary. Here are a few ideas to get you started:

- Look at cute puppy pictures or online videos.

- Fantasize about your last beach vacation. Imagine how refreshing it felt sinking into the cool, blue water.

- Play with your furry friend.

- Listen to your favorite song, turn it up, and sing or dance like nobody's listening or watching.

- Look at cute baby pictures, your own or online.

- Call your bestie to share a funny story.

These are just ideas. Create your own list and keep it handy.

> **TIP**: According to David Schwartz in *The Magic of Thinking Big*, "when you write on paper, you 'write' on your mind too."[18] Start a Gratitude Journal. List everything you're grateful for and read it regularly. This positivity exercise helps eliminate limiting beliefs and negative thoughts. Remember that all thoughts are magnetic.

Bad days are inevitable, how we choose to respond to them determines our overall mood and well-being. By implementing the strategies you learned above and adopting a positive mindset, you can transform a bad day into a relatively good one. It's not about denying or suppressing negative emotions, but rather acknowledging them and actively choosing to focus on the positive aspects of life. With practice and commitment, you will be able to find the silver lining in no time.

Closing Notes

If something is meant for you, it will come to you. Exude positive vibes, energy, and enthusiasm. Stay strong. Visualize success. Let go of doubts. Put your order into the universe. Eradicate limiting beliefs. Avoid resistance. Let life happen. Repeat: "What's meant for me will easily come to me." Envision. Believe. Be patient. Have faith. Prepare to receive. Thoughts are magnetic. Change your thoughts, change your life.

Manifest the Life You Desire Exercises

Hopefully, you've completed the tasks discussed in this chapter. Now:

- Spend ten minutes each day mentally envisioning the images you've created of your ideal life. Remember to *feel* what it's like to materialize the things you want.

- Think about a bad day you had recently. Can you mentally go through the scenario that day and reframe how you could have turned the situation around?

- Try the "3-6-9" method. Genius inventor Nikola Tesla considered combining the numbers three, six, and nine "the key to the universe."[19] Try writing your desire statement three times in the morning, six times during the day, and nine times in the evening. At the very least, it will keep your desires in the forefront of your mind and assist with visualization and manifesting.

Principle #9: Practice Gratitude Daily

LOTUS FLOWER

Description: Because a lotus flower rises from the mud and opens anew each day, it represents purity, rebirth, and renewal. Think of a lotus flower when seeking a spiritual awakening or expansion of your soul through meditation and insight, retaining purity of spirit through life's challenges.

Mantras:

I am grateful for who I am and what I have.

I honor myself and my many blessings.

I am forever being reborn anew.

My soul is strong and pure.

Inspirational Song: "Thank You," by Kehlani. Be grateful for all that you have and remember those who helped you along the way. Express gratitude to yourself and others.

Opening Notes

Gratitude can change the world. It's a mindset that can bring about complete happiness and joy. Learning how to be grateful can alter our lives. When we embrace thankfulness and gratitude, we obtain a feeling of purpose, feel closer to people, and gravitate toward authenticity and optimism. In showing gratitude, we honor ourselves and others.

In the mid-1990s, I became a single parent with a three-year-old and a newborn baby girl. Luckily for me, I had completed almost two years of college during my seven years in the U.S. Marine Corps, but I still didn't have a degree. To provide the life my daughters deserved, I had to complete college while working full time. Fortunately, everything I learned in the Marine Corps gave me the commitment, courage, and honor to do what I had to do—no matter how hard it often proved to be.

Some days I left at 6:30 a.m. and didn't return home till 10:15 p.m. I'd pick my girls up from my mom's house after class, take them home, get them to bed, study for an hour, ready everything for the next day, then hit the sack exhausted. This schedule went on for two straight years.

Two years later I earned a Bachelor of Science in Business, and life began to change for our little family. Little more than a year later, I decided to pursue a Master of

Business Administration (MBA). I loved learning and setting an example for my girls to follow. Luckily, my family helped this time too, and they celebrated along with me when I received my diploma. I felt so grateful for their support.

Nevertheless, as my girls got older, I wondered what came after those intensive parenting duties waned. I felt like I was drifting through life without a clear direction. I read books about finding purpose, researched, took tests, and self-analyzed constantly, but I still felt stuck on a "what-am-I-here-for" spinning wheel. It kept me up at night, and the longer it went on, the more discouraged I felt.

Sound familiar?

It wasn't until I learned to stop pressuring myself to meet a self-created timeline and live each day with intention and gratitude that things began to change . . . slowly. I did the work required to find a new passion with courage and commitment, honored myself and my process, visualized success, and believed with all my heart that my dreams would come true. It proved easier than you might think and removed all that self-inflicted pressure many of us experience.

"When I started counting my blessings,
my whole life turned around."

—**Willie Nelson, musician**

Be Mindfully Present

Mindfully enjoying the moment is instrumental for your mental well-being. When you physically, mentally, and emotionally engage in what's happening in the present moment, you'll be far more focused. Intentional focus also bolsters self-awareness and builds better relationships. It also helps you feel gratitude for the small moments in life that bring joy.

Shifting your focus to the present and what you currently have in your life, versus what you don't have, is as simple as flipping a switch in your mind. It's a simple decision you make. For instance, instead of constantly saying, "I wish I had a new car," or "All my friends have nicer, newer cars," flip that switch and *decide* to say, "I am grateful that I have a reliable car that gets me back and forth to work each day." The universe is more attentive to this type of reframing—because it is focused on gratitude. If you focus on being grateful for your many blessings, you develop a positivity mindset that bolsters your ability to manifest what you want in life.

Think of gratitude as a muscle you can develop.

Here are three examples of how you can live mindfully present and practice gratitude:

1. Tell someone at work how much you appreciate them. Write them a handwritten "thank you" note or offer to treat them to a fancy coffee from the local coffee shop. Email their boss to express how much you appreciate your colleague's work. Make sure you copy the colleague so he or she can also see your heartfelt appreciation. Make it a regular practice.

2. When your children are with you, put your phone away and pay attention to them. Don't worry about Instagram, Facebook, or TikTok. Those platforms will always be there. Being fully present for your children is a priceless gift for all of you. Be grateful for the time you have to share with them and focus on making the most of it. Tell them how much you love being their parent.

3. If you have adult children, plan a dinner or fun event with each of them so you can offer individual attention. Don't wait for a once-a-year birthday. My friend has four young adult sons with whom she has planned dinners, bike rides, 10k races, and even a backpacking adventure out west. Make it your intention to offer each child your

full attention. Be mindfully present and both feel and express gratitude for the joy you feel.

For me, being mindfully present and both feeling and expressing gratitude were skills I wanted to foster. To improve, I had to *intentionally* slow down the pace of life and identify the many big and small blessings I had in my life.

After returning from a family vacation, my seventy-four-year-old mother became extremely sick and ended up in the hospital for eleven days. My sole purpose during those eleven days was ensuring she received proper care and making sure she saw a familiar face every day. Purpose doesn't always have to be something grand. It can be as simple as being there for someone when they need you. I felt grateful to be retired and available to be her advocate when she needed me most.

During her recovery, I focused on living with more intention and gratitude each day. I began taking my mom on walks, playing memory games, and taking her out to run errands. I loved to see her smile as we lived in those moments. Because I focused on being mindfully present, living with intention, and expressing gratitude, I experienced a whole new thought process. As Mom improved and I resumed writing this book, ideas flowed more freely.

When you are mindfully present and live your life

with intention and gratitude, the path you're headed on shifts. You might not be 100% sure where you're going, but you're headed in a positive direction. Why? In *Your Best Year Ever*, Michael Hyatt suggests that "gratitude moves us into a place of abundance, a place where we're more resourceful, creative, generous optimistic, and kind."[20]

> *"In ordinary life, we hardly realize that we receive a great deal more than we give and that it is only with gratitude that life becomes rich."*
>
> **—Dietrich Bonhoeffer, theologian**

Imagine that you're out with your significant other on a date, and when you arrive at the dimly lit restaurant, the hostess sits you at a table near the kitchen door, which incessantly opens and closes. The bright light of the kitchen detracts from the ambiance, and you immediately feel a little irritated. Getting a glass of water takes forever. They are out of the dish you had been thinking about since the day you made your reservation. The night is not going as planned, and your irritation is growing.

Now *stop*. Let's reframe this. Imagine feeling grateful to have a wonderful person sitting opposite you who loves and cares for you. Feel grateful that you chatted with friends you hadn't seen in a long while on the way back to that table near the kitchen, and now you're happy because you arranged to meet up with those friends for drinks later that night.

By focusing on gratitude, you learn to focus on what's good in your life, and the more you do that, the more likely you will manifest what you want in life. You often can't change what happens, but you can change how you think and react.

> *"Do not spoil what you have by desiring what you have not. Remember that what you now have was once among the things you only hoped for."*
>
> **—Epicurus, ancient philosopher**

Promote Positivity

When an elderly Pennsylvania woman named Joan Lewis received a terminal diagnosis, she immediately told family and friends to not make a fuss: "Just do something nice for somebody else. Then tell me about it," she said.[21]

Over time, across continents, people heard about Joan's story. Word of kind deeds soon came almost every day, and Joan enjoyed reading about them. They lifted her spirits like nothing else could.

"An acquaintance of mine didn't have enough to eat the past few weeks, so I stopped off with a few bags of groceries," wrote one person. "I gave my co-worker a hug in your honor this morning," said another.[22]

A month after being told that her cancer had spread, reducing her predicted lifespan to weeks or even days, Joan felt well enough to try activities she had previously only dreamed of doing (her *bucket* list of items!). She flew in a hot-air balloon, stayed at a fancy hotel in Manhattan, and enjoyed a taping of her favorite daytime show. Weeks turned into months, and months turned into a year. Joan's optimistic attitude, heartfelt gratitude, and the outpouring of positivity from complete strangers enabled her to hang on long enough to undergo medical treatment. Miraculously, one year turned into eighteen months.

"These last eighteen months have been like Tom Sawyer's funeral, a chance to hear and be surprised by people thanking me for affecting them," Joan Lewis reported. "I am so blessed, the luckiest woman on Earth, really. I especially love the notes that tell me what charitable deeds people have done in honor of 'Joannie from Pringle.'"[23]

"Appreciation can make a day, even change your life. Your willingness to put into words is all that is necessary."

—**Margaret Cousins, suffragist, theosophist**

Relish Small Moments

Imagine what life would be like if we all did something nice for somebody once a week or noticed when something good happened to us. Do you ever pause to fully appreciate the smell of a fresh pot of coffee, or a beautiful, fiery sunset on a cold evening? We often fail to notice and be grateful for these small moments, which was the whole point of Thornton Wilder's play *Our Town*.[24]

The play depicts early 1900s American life and focuses on love, marriage, and death within two families. Emily and George, children from these families, marry as teenagers. Emily dies giving birth to a second child and becomes one of the wandering dead who gather at the cemetery to lament their lives. When she wants to revisit her twelfth birthday, her companions tell her it will only make her sad.

But Emily chooses to relive the moment. As an observer, Emily notices that her mother never looks at her. By the end of the play, it's obvious that the living are often blind to what matters and how short their time on earth is. Going back proved pointless because Emily was not able to change anyone's path.

The real message is that every moment is precious. We don't know what tomorrow will bring. Living a life of commitment, courage, and honor is one way to ensure that you are also living a life with a grateful and kind heart.

Create Your Own Hallmark Moments to Relish

As happens when you have more than one child, my first daughter ended up with two *Baby's First Christmas* Hallmark ornaments. Regrettably, daughter number two never received even one. Each year we decorated the Christmas tree, she would ask, "Mom, where's my *Baby's First Christmas* ornament?" By the time she was ten, she didn't accept my flimsy excuses and expressed resentment about the situation. I felt guilty.

I searched everywhere for a 1993 *Baby's First Christmas* Hallmark ornament, but it proved difficult. A few days before Christmas, I finally found and ordered one. I had zero expectations of receiving it before Christmas and planned to save it for the following year.

Christmas morning finally arrived that year, and we were all busy opening gifts. About halfway through opening presents, the doorbell rang. I thought, wow, Grandma is early this year. To my surprise, the UPS man delivered a package, and it soon resembled a scene from *A Christmas Vacation* with Chevy Chase. When Kaitlyn realized she was finally getting her Hallmark ornament, she smiled from ear to ear. That $15 ornament became the best gift she received that year, and boy was she grateful. In the end, it gave us a Christmas memory that will last a lifetime.

Carpe Diem, Latin for "seize the day," has earned a reputation as a timeless motto. The idea urges us to live with gratitude, intention, and purpose and to make the most of our time. In a world that constantly urges us to rush forward, it is essential to pause and reflect on the preciousness of every moment. By finding beauty in the ordinary, living mindfully, cultivating gratitude, and seizing the day, we can transform our lives into an array of cherished memories and unforgettable moments.

Use the Power of Words

To bolster your gratitude mindset, create a phrase that will inspire you to be your best self, no matter what you are doing in life. Here are some examples for inspiration:

- Enjoy the journey.
- Be fiercely courageous.
- Stay committed.
- Honor myself.

- Be intentional.
- Stay strong.
- Be happy.
- Practice positivity.
- Always choose kindness.
- Be a faithful friend.
- Stay the course.
- Never give up.
- I believe in me.
- Miles to go.
- Smile today.
- Don't wait for the good stuff.

Write your phrase down in your journal or on sticky notes that you put in prominent places, or have it engraved on a bracelet and wear it daily to remind you what's profoundly important, particularly when life gets a little crazy.

Janice Kaplan, author of *The Gratitude Diaries* noticed the actor Daniel Craig wearing an engraved bracelet that said: "The more joy we have, the more nearly perfect we are." Craig told Kaplan that he wore it because he loved the idea that joy is what makes you perfect. "It's a good philosophy to get you through life, isn't it?" Craig asked.[25]

It is a brilliant philosophy. No matter who you are or what you do for a living, sometimes we all need reminders to tamp down self-doubt, slow us down a bit, or help us stay the course.

There is a small lunch spot in my hometown called The Garden Bar. Every time you order a meal, they slip a handwritten, inspirational note onto your plate. It's a small gesture that always brings a little smile to my face. It's The Garden Bar's way of showing gratitude that you spent your hard-earned money at their establishment, particularly when you have many other options to choose from.

Closing Notes

Gratitude is an attitude. Time is limited. Feel grateful. Say thank you. Get off your phone. Be mindfully present. Live with intention. Show kindness. Spread joy. Pay it forward. Share your smile. Be thankful for food, family, and clean water. Show up every day with a grateful heart.

Practice Gratitude Daily Exercises

To foster daily gratitude, try these exercises:

- Think of ways you can live each day with intention and gratitude. Write the ideas in your journal. Do them all.

- Tonight, before you go to bed, write about two small moments in which you were mindfully present and experienced gratitude. Create more of these moments as you go forward.

- Create and maintain a gratitude journal and write in it every night for at least six weeks or until it becomes habit.

- List potent motivational words or phrases. Choose the one that speaks most to your heart's deepest desire. Write it in your journal or on sticky notes you place around your house and view often. Even better, engrave a bracelet or pendant with your chosen word or phrase. Use it to exercise courage, commitment, and honor. You can doodle or brainstorm some ideas in the blank space below:

Principle #10:
Keep The End In Mind

CAT

Description: Cats are so self-sufficient and resilient we imagine them having nine lives. Humans only get one. One short life. Make the most of yours.

Mantras:

I love who I used to be, who I am, and who I am becoming.

Every day I grow into a better version of me.

Although I've made mistakes, they don't define me.

My vision for my future is powerful, and I deserve to expect the life of my dreams.

Inspirational Song: "Firework," by Katy Perry. You're more likely to create fireworks in your life if you keep the end in mind. Check all fear and pride at the door.

Opening Notes

"Remembering that I'll be dead soon is the most important tool I've ever encountered to help me make the big choices in life," Apple creator Steve Jobs said. *"Because almost everything— all external expectations, all pride, all fear of embarrassment or failure—these things just fall away in the face of death, leaving only what is truly important. Remembering that you are going to die is the best way I know to avoid the trap of thinking you have something to lose. You are already naked. There is no reason not to follow your heart."*[26]

Steve Jobs said the above six years before his passing, during a moving commencement speech to Stanford graduates in which one of his main themes was death. His words inspired many to be more fully aware that our lives will be short and that it's up to us to maximize what we do with them. Jobs used his approaching death as a tool to empower himself.

Why You Should Write Your Own Eulogy

The word "eulogy" is derived from the Greek word *eulogia*, which means "good words." Because we typically use a eulogy to honor a person after death, most write eulogies that provide a narrative overview of a person's life and how they lived it. The eulogy author strives to reveal the essence of a person's heart and soul.

Daniel Harkavy, author of *Living Forward*, proposed

that we write a eulogy about our own lives as motivation to change. "When we take the time to write our eulogies, it creates this magnetic pull power that draws us forward; our priorities and our vision for where we want to be as leaders and how we'll get there come into sharp focus. This clarity enables us to make the best decisions, get up out of our comfortable patterns, create new habits, and start moving toward a better future," Harkavy said.[27]

The only time most people even think about their own mortality is when they are filling out the beneficiary information on their life insurance forms or writing their will. When something goes wrong, we hate filling out those "end of life" directives. This is very human and understandable, nevertheless, we only have a short time here on earth. Thinking about that actuality may feel morbid, but it's also a way to make sure you are maximizing your time on planet Earth.

Now that you've made it to Principle #10, muster the courage to think about your life and how you would like to summarize it at the end. Doing so will allow you to gain the kind of perspective and clarity that can help you decide what you want to do with your life in the here and now. It may also create a sense of urgency that you can use to light a fire under yourself. Sometimes it even helps people decide to follow their heart.

How to Begin

To write your own eulogy, begin by recalling the most memorable and transformational moments in your life. If you need help, ask yourself the following questions:

- What have been some of your proudest moments?
- What challenges did you struggle to overcome?
- Are there any funny moments that stand out?
- What were your most loving, kind, or generous moments?
- When were you most present, engaged, or essential?
- What impact have your actions had on others?
- How might some of these situations or outcomes have been different without you?
- What do people admire most about you?

Once you've gathered everything you think matters, think about how you want to organize these thoughts.

How to Write Your Eulogy

Listed below is a six-step method you can use for writing a eulogy that will help you refocus your life:

Step 1: Visualize your funeral or wake. Who will write your eulogy and read it to those gathered?

Where might it be? Who will attend? Of those people, what might each say about what you brought to their lives? This step will get you in the right frame of mind.

Step 2: Write a eulogy for the life you are currently living. You can use a story format and interject quotes, sayings, poems, or information from others. If it feels really awkward to write your own eulogy, imagine that you are writing this solely for your most trusted friend to read. Remember, you don't ever have to show it anyone. This is essentially a progress report for your eyes only.

Step 3: Write a eulogy for the life you would have loved to live, the one that fulfills all your goals and dreams. Imagine what you would want people to say about you when you're gone, how you want people to feel about you, and what lessons you want to impart to those listening to your eulogy or seeing your eulogy in print. Here are a few more prompts to help you with this step. What was it about you that made other people admire you the most? What was it about spending time with you that brought them the most joy? What are some of the compliments that were frequently given to you? What are some instances in which you assisted other people in a way that they would remember for a long time? What is it about you that others will miss the most? This is your legacy eulogy. This is the life you lived with commitment, courage, and honor. You are proud of this life.

Step 4: Read each eulogy aloud. If your legacy eulogy doesn't pull heartstrings and elicit strong emotion, ask yourself why and refine it, if necessary.

Step 5: Compare the two eulogies and notice where you are now and where you'd like to be.

Step 6: What insight did these exercises provide about the meaning you want out of life? What changes do you need to make in your life now to start living a life of commitment, courage, and honor?

The hard part is now done. Take advantage of this life-changing insight and act on your clarified goals and dreams, as depicted in the legacy eulogy created in step 3. You might even be able to create new bucket list items from what you've written in your eulogy.

To give you an idea of how to start your own, here's the short version legacy eulogy I wrote for myself after completing the six steps above:

Tamara was a devoted wife, mom, grandmother, daughter, friend, and true lover of life. She loved reading and learning about innovative ideas.

When Tamara found something to pursue, she pursued it with pure passion and childlike excitement, and it showed. She frequently breezed past her comfort zone and encouraged others to do the same. She knew that getting out of her comfort zone was where the true magic happened.

Her biggest passion was helping others live a life of commitment, courage, and honor—three values she learned during her time with the United States Marines. Tamara lived her life to the fullest, always choosing happiness, following her dreams, setting and achieving goals, and having a bucket list that she heartily fulfilled. Her curious nature took her around the world, where she met friends while also collecting thousands of memorable experiences. Her life was filled with love, adventure, travel, giving back, fun, and laughter. She fiercely loved her husband, children, and grandchildren. Tamara touched the hearts of many, and her biggest achievement was knowing she made a difference and left this world a better place. Oh, and did I mention she was brutally competitive and hated losing but softened as the years went by?

Writing your eulogy is a transformative practice that empowers us to live with purpose, clarity, and intention by allowing you to reflect on the person you hope to become and the legacy you want to leave behind. Use it as a blueprint for your future. Take a moment to envision your desired future, and let that vision guide your actions towards a life well-lived.

Closing Notes

We have but one life to live. Live life to the fullest. Keep the end in mind. Take time to reflect. Leave a legacy. Time is valuable. Live a regret-free life. Create and then celebrate memorable moments. What will people say about you? What do you want people to say about you?

Keep the End in Mind Exercises

Complete the following tasks:

- Recall the most memorable and transformational moments in your life so far. Write about them in your journal.

- Write about how it felt to compose your current and your legacy eulogies.

- List any changes you will make now that you have a new vision of what your life could be.

- Was this chapter uncomfortable or was it a wakeup call? Write about this in your journal.

Conclusion

The fact that you've read this book and we're not close friends or family means I got out of my comfort zone, I set SMART as HELL goals for myself, and I put one foot in front of the other until this book became reality—a dream come true.

Did I always believe in myself? Absolutely not. I had overwhelming feelings of doubt, anxiety about not being smart enough, fear of failure and rejection, and wondering if anyone would read a book I wrote. Could I even figure out how to get this book into your hands? On Veteran's Day 2022, I put out a Facebook post on my personal page that said:

"Happy Veteran's Day to all my fellow veterans! I thought this would be the perfect day to say that I am in the process of writing a book, which starts with my time in the USMC back in 1984. It's a self-help book about living your life with commitment, courage, and honor. It covers goal setting, being grateful, finding your passions and unique talents, following your values, facing your fears and getting out of your comfort zone (like I'm doing in this post, ha, ha), having a bucket list and completing activities on that list, starting with the end in mind, and having a fit body and mind. This is my way of holding myself accountable. I have joined a writer's group at the Grove City Library where there are several published authors, and my confidence is growing daily. Super excited as this goal has been on my radar for quite some time."

The post put me on the spot in public forum. I really committed to punching my fear in the face and telling the universe, I'm on my way and there's no stopping me now. Then I mustered the courage required and got to work, honoring my goal of writing a self-help book in the hope that what I have learned throughout my life can help many others.

The world needs your unique gifts, never forget that. Continue to grow. The process of growth is both beautiful and rewarding. There will be times when you will need to look back and remember being on the verge of giving up, when you felt truly threatened, or when you worried yourself sick over a situation. Remember, you got through every one of them. When you can look at yourself in the mirror and acknowledge that you gave it your all, you've come full circle. Be proud of those moments.

. . . .

You are the only person in this world who will never leave your side, so invest in you.

. . . .

You are transitioning into a newer version of yourself, replacing an older one that is no longer relevant. Have patience with yourself as you change, transform, reinvent, and develop. My wish for you is that this book will give you the tools you need to live a joyful life. Countless people, family, friends, inspirational books, and real-life stories have made my life just a little bit better, and I hope I can do the same for you. My wish for you is to live a life of commitment, courage, and honor every single day because life is too short to waste a single day. Join the movement of women who are setting and committing to hard goals, gaining confidence, and thriving. Together, let's make this chapter the most empowering and fulfilling one of your life. Ignite your inner compass.

As my fellow Marines would say, "Ooh-rah!"

"Two roads diverged in a wood, and I—
I took the one less traveled by, and that
has made all the difference."

—Robert Frost, poet

Acknowledgments

Thanks to my husband, Greg. Honestly, he is by far my biggest cheerleader. I have had many side hustles in my life, and he always encouraged and supported me. He was my IT support, the person I bounced ideas off, the person who in 2021 bought me an on-line coaching session with Jen Sincero six months before my retirement. He knew I had ideas I needed to share with the world, probably even before I did. Greg was the one who believed in me and made me realize I was so much more than where I started.

I'd also like to thank my first two beta readers, Breanne Adkins and Megan Paxman, for providing me with advice and guidance on ways to make this book even better.

Thank you to my developmental editor, Susan Reynolds, my copy editor Lois Greenlee Stück, proofreader D. Baldogo, and my cover and book designer Susan Malikowski.

Thank you to my mentors, whom I have yet to meet, nonetheless, they have been inspirational to me for quite some time. These people include Oprah Winfrey, Zig Ziglar, Napoleon Hill, Norman Vincent Peale, David Schwartz, Jen Sincero, Brené Brown, Eleanor Roosevelt, Mel Robbins, Rhonda Byrne, and Suze

Orman. Thank you for inspiring me to be more and for paving the way.

If you found my book enjoyable and valuable, the greatest compliment you can offer as a reader is to leave a review on Amazon. Your feedback and support through an honest review can have a significant impact on an author like myself. Taking a few moments to share your thoughts on Amazon not only encourages other potential readers but also helps me as an author grow and improve. Your review is truly appreciated and means the world to me. Thank you for considering this gesture of support!

Field Guide Notes and Drawings

Notes

Principle #1

1   Angela Duckworth, *Grit* (New York: Scribner, 2016), 103.

2   Brit Morse, "These Founders Hit the Road—and Found Their Next Big Idea," *Inc.* November 6, 2017, https://www.inc.com/brit-morse/pandemic-mothers-forced-leave-jobs-company-leasecake.html.

3   Ibid.

Principle #2

4   Laura Morgan Roberts, Gretchen Spreitzer, Jane Dutton, Robert E. Quinn, Emily D. Heaphy, and Brianna Barker, "How t o Play to Your Strengths," *Harvard Business Review*, January 2005, https://hbr.org/2005/01/how-to-play-to-your-strengths.

Principle #3

5   Jenny Blake, *Pivot* (New York: Penguin Random House, 2016), 41.

6   Jenny Blake, *Life After College* (Philadelphia: Running Press, 2011), 27

Principle #4

7   Judith Bardwick, quoted by Oliver Page, "How to Leave Your Comfort Zone and Enter Your 'Growth Zone,'" *Positive Psychology*, November 4, 2020, https://positivepsychology.com/comfort-zone/.

8   Bronnie Ware, *The Top Five Regrets of the Dying* (Carlsbad, CA: Hay House, 2019), 44.

9   Steven Pressfield, *The War of Art: Break Through the Blocks and Win Your Inner Creative Battle*s (New York: Black Irish Entertainment, 2012), 40.

Principle #6

10   Read Caleb Williams's full Heisman Trophy speech, "Just Keep Believing," *Los Angeles Times*, December 10, 2022, https://www.latimes.com/sports/usc/story/2022-12-10/read-it-caleb-williams-heisman-trophy-speech.

11   George T. Doran, "There's a S.M.A.R.T. Way to Write Management's Goals and Objectives," accessed February 12, 2023, https://community.mis.temple.edu/mis0855002fall2015/files/2015/10/S.M.A.R.T-Way-Management-Review.pdf.

12   "My Personal Vision Board," *Jack Canfield*, accessed November 30, 2022, https://jackcanfield.com/blog/my-personal-vision-board/.

13   Matt Chivers, "Tiger Woods Describes Putting Visualisation Technique in Classic Footage," *Golf Magic*, July 29, 2021, https://www.golfmagic.com/golf-news/tiger-woods-describes-putting-visualisation-technique-classic-footage.

14   "What Oprah Learned from Jim Carrey," *OWN*, October 12, 2011, https://www.oprah.com/oprahs-lifeclass/what-oprah-learned-from-jim-carrey-video.

15   Arman Suleimenov, "Bruce Lee's Definite Chief Aim in Life," *Medium*, October 24, 2013, https://medium.com/@suleimenov/the-bruce-lees-definite-chief-aim-in-life-ba035009548c.

16   David Goggins, *Can't Hurt Me: Master Your Mind and Defy the Odds* (Austin, TX: Lioncrest Publishing, 2018).

17   "Lincoln's Failure List," Abraham Lincoln Online, accessed November 2, 2022, https://www.abrahamlincolnonline.org/lincoln/education/failures.htm.

Principle #8

18   David J. Schwartz, Ph.D., *The Magic of Thinking Big* (New York: Simon & Schuster, 1987), 143.

19   Sarah Regan, "The 369 Manifestation Method Is Super Popular—But Does It Work?" *MBGMindfulness*, July 29, 2021, https://www.mindbodygreen.com/articles/369-manifestation-method.

Principle #9

20   Michael Hyatt, *Your Best Year Ever* (Grand Rapids, MI: Baker Books, 2018), 92.

21   Sally Deneen, "If You Were Dying ... Would Gratitude Be Your First Thought?" *Success*, November 16, 2022, https://www.success.com/if-you-were-dying-would-gratitude-be-your-first-thought/.

22   Ibid.

23   Ibid.

24   "Our Town Summary," SoftSchools.com, accessed October 21, 2022, https://www.softschools.com/literature/summary/our_town/.

25 Janice Kaplan, *The Gratitude Diaries: How a Year Looking on the Bright Side Can Transform Your Life* (New York: Dutton, 2015), 138.

Principle #10

26 Steve Jobs's commencement address, quoted in "'You've got to find what you love,' Jobs says," *Stanford News*, June 12, 2005, https://news.stanford.edu/2005/06/12/youve-got-find-love-jobs-says/.

27 Michael Grothaus, "How vividly imaging your own death can help your next career move," *Fast Company*, November 16, 2018, https://www.fastcompany.com/90266043/how-vividly-imagining-your-own-death-can-help-your-next-career-move.

www.ingramcontent.com/pod-product-compliance
Lightning Source LLC
Chambersburg PA
CBHW020243130626
46549CB00005B/2032